Pascal Simplified

Pascal Simplified
A Guide for
the First-Time User

SUSAN H. GRAY

New York Institute of Technology

Rowman & Allanheld

PUBLISHERS

ROWMAN & ALLANHELD

Published in the United States of America in 1986
by Rowman & Allanheld, Publishers
(a division of Littlefield, Adams & Company)
81 Adams Drive, Totowa, New Jersey 07512

Library of Congress Cataloging in Publication Data

Gray, Susan H.
  Pascal simplified.

  Includes indexes.
  1. PASCAL (Computer program language)   I. Title.
QA76.73.P2G74   1986   005.13'3   85-14197
ISBN 0-8476-7428-2
ISBN 0-8226-0394-2 (pbk.)

86 87 88/10 9 8 7 6 5 4 3 2 1

Printed in the United States of America

To my parents, Ben and Sophie Case,
and to Eric Hoffmann

Table of Contents

Preface

This book is designed for a one-semester course in Pascal or for the person who is learning to work with Pascal for the first time. It is intended primarily for those who have had no previous exposure to a computer language or those looking for a simplified approach to Pascal. Courses in Pascal are being taught in more and more colleges and universities. A version of Pascal related to the standard version taught here can be used in programming many personal computers—for example, Apple computers, the IBM PC, Kaypro and Tandy/Radio Shack computers.

This book covers all major aspects of Standard Pascal. Basic material introduced in the early chapters is presented on a fundamental instructional level. More advanced material in later chapters is also presented in simplified form, but the programs and review exercises are more complex.

Each chapter is a separate study unit that contains illustrative programs and program segments. Additional exercises with answers are found at the end of each chapter. The answers to the review exercises are not the *only* correct answers. Everyone has his or her individual programming style, and in most cases there are several approaches to writing a useful program. The answers are suggestions, designed to illustrate the concepts introduced in that chapter.

Illustrative programs, program segments, and syntactic forms appearing in programs are capitalized to set them off from the rest of the text. This is designed to make the text more readable and to enable you to locate more quickly applications of the syntactic rules for writing Pascal programs. In syntactic rules, parts of program text to be filled in by the programmer are underlined to distinguish them from reserved words and standard identifiers in Pascal.

1

Introduction

Computers are simply machines that store and manipulate information. They may be as simple as a hand-held calculator or as complex as a mainframe that fills an entire room. But this book assumes that you are interested in learning to use something in between—a desktop home or business computer or a small mainframe computer.

All computers have four components in common:

1. *Memory.* Information is stored in the memory of the computer. Also stored in memory is the set of instructions for manipulating this information. In personal computers, diskettes and tapes can also provide auxiliary storage of information and programs, but these must be entered into memory from the disk or tape before they can be used and manipulated. The memory storage that holds the programs and information in a personal computer is called RAM, or random access memory.

2. *Input Device.* The input device, e.g., the keyboard, enables you to enter data and instructions into memory.

3. *CPU,* or Central Processing Unit. The CPU can access information (data or instructions) from memory, perform computations, and store the information in memory. Computers are unique because of the power of the CPU. The CPU can perform computations and coordinate all the functions of the

computer, but it can also logically compare information and make decisions based on that information.

4. *Output Device.* The output device enables you to retrieve and display information in memory, either the result of a computation or simply the original data that you entered. A monitor, a television screen without the tuner, is one way of displaying output, text or graphics. A printer interfaced with the computer produces a paper copy of the output.

Programming Languages

Computers follow a set of instructions written in the form of a *program* and are written in a *programming language.* The language has a vocabulary and grammar, but they are much more precise than English. If you ever saw Mel Brooks's movie "Young Frankenstein," you may remember the joke in which Igor says to Dr. Frankenstein, "Walk this way." Instead of walking in the direction indicated, Dr. Frankenstein imitates Igor's peculiar movements. This is an example of the ambiguities that can occur in English. A programming language has to be more precise because a computer will, like Igor, follow your exact instructions, even when you make a mistake. The computer may follow your instructions correctly but produce an incorrect result because of your own error. The computer might also send you an *error message* saying that it cannot follow your instructions.

Computers do not read programs directly. The programming language that your program is written in is translated into binary codes that the computer can understand (*machine language*). Programs are usually written in a programming language rather than machine language because programming languages are easier to write in and are applicable to a wider variety of computers.

For example, one way of representing in machine language the word "Hello" (if you wanted to have your computer write "Hello" to you) is the series:

```
01001000
01100101
01101100
01101100
01101111
```

These rows of binary codes each represent one of the letters in the word "Hello." In Pascal, if you want the computer to print "Hello," you can use the instruction Writeln ('Hello');.

Pascal is one of several of the high-level computer programming languages. This means that it is both sophisticated and powerful. It was developed by Niklaus Wirth in 1971 and named after the seventeenth-century philosopher Blaise Pascal. Although there are several versions of Pascal, an attempt has been made to standardize the language in a form known as Standard Pascal.

Algorithms: Constructing a Program Outline

I remember a brand of canned food that could be bought in the supermarket when I was younger that came with the instructions:

1. Open the can
2. Put the contents of the can in a pot
3. Heat the contents
4. Serve the contents

I used to be amused by these instructions because it seemed that opening the can was such an obvious first step. But when instructing a computer, you *must* specify the obvious. The instructions for preparing the can of food are a primitive form of an *algorithm*; that is, a sequence of steps made up of logical operations designed to solve a problem, in this case serving a can of food.

Suppose, for example, that you want the computer to find the sum of two numbers. Let's suppose that each number has a name, NUMBER1 and NUMBER2, but you do not yet know their values. You want the instructions to the computer to be general instructions for any two numbers.

Before constructing an algorithm, think first about how you will name items of information for the computer, in this case the two numbers, NUMBER1 and NUMBER2, and the sum. Let's call the sum ANSWER.

To find the sum, follow these steps:

1. Read the information that is input (the two numbers)
2. Place that information into NUMBER1 and NUMBER2
3. Compute the sum of the numbers in NUMBER1 and NUMBER2
4. Place the result of the summation in ANSWER
5. Display the number stored in ANSWER

Notice how you begin by putting information into named variables and end by writing information out from a named variable. (This writing or printing may take place only on the monitor at this point.)

The steps of an algorithm sometimes must be further refined and clarified. For example, "open the can" may not be specific enough, and you may have to break down the instruction into a detailed sequence of steps. This is the program-formulation process. The algorithm is refined until all steps are clear. The steps are then followed to make sure that the instructions for the algorithm contain no logical errors. The steps are then translated into a programming language, in this case Pascal.

Types of Input and Output: Naming Program Constants and Variables

To get the computer to find the sum of two numbers, the first thing you do is to name items of information. You named

both the *input* information given to the computer (the variables
NUMBER1 and NUMBER2) and the *output* information that
the computer gives back (the variable ANSWER).

Variables and Constants

NUMBER1, NUMBER2, and ANSWER are *variables* because
they can take on a variety of values. NUMBER1 may be 7 or
3.2, for example, and ANSWER will vary accordingly. Items
of information may also be *constants*—values that don't change.
You must name and define all of the constants and variables in
your program before the computer can execute the sequence of
steps.

If your program contains a constant, you can assign its value
in the statement that defines the constant. For example, suppose that each of the numbers that you wish to sum is to be
adjusted by the addition of a constant equal to 2. Let's name
this constant INCREASE. All of the names that you use for
constants are *identifiers* and therefore must:

1. Contain only letters of the alphabet and the numbers 0
   through 9
2. Begin with a letter of the alphabet
3. *Not* be a reserved word, such as CONST and VAR. (A
   complete list of reserved words follows.) Reserved words
   have a predefined meaning. Their uses will be discussed
   in later chapters.
4. Some compilers will use only the first eight letters and
   numbers of your constant name.

For example, the computer will not be able to read
$INCREASE, 3INCREASE, or DIV as labels because the first
two words do not begin with a letter of the alphabet. The last
is a reserved word.

Reserved Words in Standard Pascal

```
AND
ARRAY
BEGIN
CASE
CONST
DIV
DO
DOWNTO
ELSE
END
FILE
FOR
FUNCTION
GOTO
IF
IN
LABEL
MOD
NIL
NOT
OF
OR
PACKED
PROCEDURE
PROGRAM
RECORD
REPEAT
SET
THEN
TO
TYPE
UNTIL
VAR
WHILE
WITH
```

Avoid using predefined or predeclared identifiers as names for constants or variables, because doing so will make your program more difficult to read. These identifiers include:

```
BOOLEAN
CHAR
FALSE
INPUT
INTEGER
MAXINT
OUTPUT
REAL
TEXT
TRUE
```

Others are described in Chapter 5.

To name the constant INCREASE, type in:

```
CONST
  INCREASE = 2;
```

CONST alerts the computer to expect a definition of a constant (or several constants) to follow. The constant is then equated with a value. Remember this as:

```
CONST
  CONSTANT-NAME = CONSTANT-VALUE;
```

You can fill in CONSTANT-NAME and CONSTANT-VALUE with any valid identifier and value, respectively. Remember that you cannot change the value of any constant in your program.

Note that the syntactic form for a line of instruction for your computer ends with a semicolon. This semicolon separates each statement from the one that follows. A semicolon is not used after CONST and before INCREASE because they are part of the same statement and could be written on the same line. They are separated here to make the statement easier to read.

Next, you must define the variables. Defining a variable is more complex than defining a constant. Since variables change in value, they are not assigned a value in their definition statement. Rather, while the program is *executing*—that is, while the computer is following your instructions—the data in each variable will be stored in memory.

Variable definition statements tell the computer what type of data to expect for each variable. The four basic data types are integer, real, char, and Boolean.

Integer and Real Data Types

The basic data types, as well as other data types that you can define, will be discussed more fully in Chapter 4. For now, let's just distinguish between integer and real. In the previous example, NUMBER1, NUMBER2, and ANSWER contained numeric values. Numbers can be either *integer* or *real*. Integer values are whole numbers. They do not have a decimal point. Real values include a decimal point and are therefore used to represent quantities that may not have only whole values, such as 7.35, −10.126, or 131.0. Let's assume that NUMBER1, NUMBER2, and ANSWER contain *real* numbers.

The rules for naming constants apply to variables as well, since variables are also identifiers. (Remember that identifiers use only letters of the alphabet and the digits 0 through 9. The identifier should begin with a letter of the alphabet and never use a reserved word for a name.) Restrict variable names to eight letters and numbers or fewer, and avoid predefined identifiers.

To name the variables NUMBER1, NUMBER2, and ANSWER, type in:

```
VAR
  NUMBER1, NUMBER2, ANSWER : REAL;
```

VAR alerts the computer to expect a definition of a variable (or several variables) to follow. You then see the variables declared as being of a certain type, in this case *real*. Each variable name in the list is separated by a comma. End a variable list with a colon, which distinguishes a list from a data type.

If your program contains other types of variables or other real variables as well, you could continue to list them on additional lines, using the above format. Separate each line with a semicolon. Use the reserved words VAR or CONST only at the *beginning* of the list. For example:

```
CONST
  INCREASE = 2;
VAR
  NUMBER1,NUMBER2 : REAL;
  ANSWER : REAL;
  ADDEDVAR : INTEGER;
```

When naming variables and constants, select a descriptive name such as NUMBER1, rather than a name like VAR1 or A1, which you may not remember as you work with your program. Each variable name is distinct. You cannot use the same variable name for two different variable declarations because obviously the computer will not know how to interpret this. For example, the following instructions would be invalid.

```
NUMBER1 : REAL;
NUMBER1 : INTEGER;
```

Input and Output: Getting the Computer to Read and Write

Remember, before the computer can find the sum of two numbers, you have to tell it first to read the information that was *input*—in this example, NUMBER1 AND NUMBER2. After a series of steps, you also had to tell it to display the *output*—in this example, the sum stored in ANSWER. Setting up instructions for the input of variable data into memory and the output of information from memory is the basis for READLN, READ, WRITELN and WRITE statements.

READLN and READ Statements

To instruct the computer to expect two pieces of data—one to be stored in the variable NUMBER1 and the second to be stored in the variable NUMBER2—type in:

```
READLN (NUMBER1,NUMBER2);
```

When you type in data, any data located in those variables are no longer there. In other words, new input values replace the old. If you have a long input list, you might want to construct a more permanent file, particularly if you will use this input more than once. (See the Appendix to find out how to use that type of file as input.) For now, just use the keyboard. Separate each variable in the READLN statement by a comma, and enclose the entire variable list in parentheses.

Remember the general form of READLN statements as:

```
READLN (LIST OF VARIABLES INTO WHICH DATA ARE TO BE INPUT);
```

The READLN statement tells the computer in Pascal to read a line of input. After a READLN statement, the computer will skip to the next line if there is any further input. Without a list of variables, the READLN statement will also skip to the next line for further input, even if there is still more input on the current line. If you want the computer to continue on the same line of input—if there are more data following—you must use a READ statement. READ statements and READLN statements have the same form:

```
READ (LIST OF VARIABLES INTO WHICH DATA ARE TO BE INPUT);
```

Before continuing any further, make sure that you understand that you have three choices for instructing the computer to do the same thing:

(1)   `READLN (NUMBER1,NUMBER2);`

(2)   `READ (NUMBER1);`
        `READLN (NUMBER2);`

```
(3)    READ (NUMBER1);
       READ (NUMBER2);
       READLN;
```

WRITELN and WRITE Statements

WRITELN and WRITE statements take the same form as READLN and READ statements:

```
WRITELN (LIST OF VARIABLES CONTAINING OUTPUT);
WRITE (LIST OF VARIABLES CONTAINING OUTPUT);
```

If you want several pieces of output to be printed on separate lines, use separate WRITELN statements. If you want the output printed on a continuous line, use the WRITE statement or one continuous WRITELN statement. For example, if you want NUMBER1, NUMBER2, and ANSWER displayed on the same line, type in:

```
WRITE (NUMBER1);
WRITE (NUMBER2);
WRITE (ANSWER);
WRITELN;
```

or

```
WRITELN (NUMBER1,NUMBER2,ANSWER);
```

If you want each to be displayed on a separate line, use separate WRITELN statements:

```
WRITELN (NUMBER1);
WRITELN (NUMBER2);
WRITELN (ANSWER);
```

The WRITELN statement without a list of variables is also a convenient way of skipping a line—that is, inserting a blank line into your program output.

When instructing the computer to display output, label the output in the display and enclose the labels in single quotation marks:

```
'SUM = '
```

Include those labels in a WRITELN or WRITE statement like this:

```
WRITELN ('SUM = ', ANSWER);
```

Labels enclosed in single quotation marks are separated from a variable name, a variable list, or another label by a comma. Material between quotation marks is printed exactly as typed, including the spaces.

Readable Output

The output is displayed in *scientific notation.* If the sum of NUMBER1 and NUMBER2 were 100.0, for example, the output would be displayed on the screen as:

```
1.00000E+2
```

The +2 means move the decimal place two places to the right. You can eliminate scientific notation by allocating a specific number of columns to print any numerical output in your WRITELN or WRITE statements next to each variable name. For example, to tell the computer to end ANSWER twelve spaces from the beginning of the line and to include three decimal places, type in:

```
WRITELN (ANSWER:12:3);
```

Make sure that your first number is large enough to include the number of decimal places you want, the decimal point, and the rest of the number, as well as some leading blank spaces. ANSWER:4:3, for example, would be incorrect because it doesn't leave any room to print the part of the number preceeding the decimal point.

If several pieces of output are printed on the same line, the first number following the variable name represents the

number of spaces to the end of that piece of output from the
end of the last item written. The second number following the
variable name still indicates the number of decimal places. If
a variable is defined as *integer,* only one number—representing
the total number of spaces to the end of that piece of output—
should be included. For example, to space output across a line,
type in the statement:

```
WRITELN(NUMBER1:9:2,NUMBER2:9:2,INTEG:5,ANSWER:11:2);
```

The integer number in INTEG will end five spaces from the
last digit of NUMBER2.

Assignment Statements: Getting the Computer to Perform Computations and Manipulate Values

In the example we have been working with in this chapter, two
numbers—NUMBER1 and NUMBER2—are added to produce
a sum stored in the variable ANSWER. We have already seen
how to define the variables, read input into the appropriate
variables and then print output from the appropriate variable.
In this section you will learn how to perform the computation
after reading the input and how to place the result of the computation into ANSWER so that output can then be displayed
from ANSWER.

To add NUMBER1 and NUMBER2 and store the result in
ANSWER, use the assignment statement:

```
ANSWER := NUMBER1 + NUMBER2;
```

The variable to the left of the symbols := is the variable in
which you want the value of the right-hand side of the statement stored. If NUMBER1 and NUMBER2 are *real,* then
ANSWER also must be declared as real. Otherwise, you will
have an ungrammatical assignment statement. You cannot
assign incompatible information to a variable. Integer values

in Pascal, however, are treated as having a decimal part of zero and can be assigned to real variables. For example, if NUMBER3 is declared as integer, a valid assignment statement would be:

```
NUMBER2 := NUMBER1 + NUMBER3;
```

An assignment statement is defined by the symbols :=. The symbol + is an *operator*. NUMBER1 and NUMBER2 are *operands*. In an assignment statement, the right-hand side of the assignment statement—everything that follows the symbols :=—can be one of three items:

1. A single operand or value (such as NUMBER1 := OLDSUM;) which would put the value of OLDSUM into NUMBER1. The value would also remain in OLDSUM.

2. An operator with an operand on each of its two sides, as in ANSWER := NUMBER1 + NUMBER2;

The operators that can be used are:

+	addition
−	subtraction
*	multiplication
/	real division
DIV	integer division—returns only the whole number part of the answer
MOD	integer division—returns only the remainder part of the answer

In Pascal, the same variable can appear on both sides of an assignment statement when updating its value:

```
ANSWER := ANSWER + NUMBER1;
```

This would add the value of NUMBER1 to the old value of ANSWER and replace the old value with the new sum.

3. A combination of operators and operands that create a more complex mathematical expression. For example:

```
ANSWER := (NUMBER1 + INCREASE) * (NUMBER2 + INCREASE);
```

Here the constant INCREASE is added to NUMBER1 and to NUMBER2. Then those two sums are multiplied to produce ANSWER. The sets of parentheses tell the computer to perform the computations within each set of parentheses first. If there are no parentheses, the priorities of computation are multiplication and division, then addition and subtraction: (*,/,DIV,MOD), then (+,−).

Program Form: Putting the Basics Into a Simple Program

You should now be ready to put all the program parts together into a simple program. The Pascal statements you have seen appear in a specified order in a program:

1. Program name (input and output file names)
2. Declaration of constants (if any)
3. Declaration of variables (if any)
4. The reserved word BEGIN
5. Program statements
6. The reserved word END followed by a period (END.)

There is no semicolon following the word BEGIN and no semicolon following the last statement before END. BEGIN and END are not separate statements; instead, they delineate the beginning and end of a list of one or more statements. Every other statement should be followed by a semicolon; otherwise the computer will not be able to read the program.

The program for summing two numbers will look like this:

```
PROGRAM ADDNUMS (INPUT,OUTPUT);
(* THIS PROGRAM ADDS TWO NUMBERS & PRINTS THE SUM *)
VAR
  NUMBER1,NUMBER2,ANSWER: REAL;
BEGIN
  READLN (NUMBER1,NUMBER2);
  ANSWER := NUMBER1 + NUMBER2;
  WRITELN ('SUM = ',ANSWER:12:3)
END.
```

This program includes several new features. The program name—ADDNUMS in this case—can be any valid identifier. INPUT or OUTPUT after the program name refers to external files. They tell the computer to expect information from either the keyboard or punched cards, if there is input, and to print a hard copy or just display the output on the screen. Not all compilers require this, so check your user's manual. (For more information on files see the Appendix.)

Comment Symbols

The description of the program enclosed in the symbols (* and *) is called a *comment*. The computer ignores comments when it translates programming language into machine language, so they can be inserted anywhere in your program. They are not set off from the statement following by a semicolon. Programmers use comments to remind themselves what the program can do step by step. With some computers, the symbols { and } are used instead, so check your user's manual.

Executing Your Program

After you create your program and enter it into the computer, a Pascal compiler translates it into machine language. If there are no *syntax* errors in your program—that is, if you have not violated any of the grammatical rules of Pascal—the translated machine code will be stored in memory and the instructions in the program will be executed. If there is a problem with the logic of these instructions, such as attempting to divide by a variable assigned a value of zero, the computer may stop in the middle of the program.

For more information on creating, editing, saving, compiling, and executing a Pascal program, refer to the manual that came with your particular system.

Review Exercises

1. Which are not legitimate labels for either constants or variables?

```
24SURVEY
BOOKLIST
WEIGHT
VAR2
REPEAT
SCORES*
```

2. Write a program that prints "GOOD MORNING, SUSAN." (Substitute your own name.)

3. Write a program to read the length of an object in feet, convert the length to meters, and print its length in both feet and meters (1 meter = 3.281 feet).

4. Convert program ADDNUMS on page 15 to a program in which a constant of 2 (INCREASE) is added to each number to be summed.

5. Eliminate the syntax errors from the program:

```
PROGRAM DEBUG (INPUT,OUTPUT) (  ' )
CONST;
  SURCHGE := 15;
VAR   ( ):
  TOTAL,TAX = REAL;
  PERSONS = INTEGER;
BEGIN   ( ):          (TAX, PERSONS);
  READLN TAX; PERSONS;
  TOTAL = TAX + SURCHG * PERSONS;
  WRITELN 'THE TOTAL TAX INTAKE IS ',TOTAL:8 : 2 )
END ,
```

Answers to Review Exercises

1. 24SURVEY, REPEAT and SCORES* are not legitimate identifiers. 24SURVEY does not begin with a letter of the alphabet. REPEAT is a reserved word. SCORES* contains a character (*) that is not a letter or a number.

2.

```
PROGRAM HELLO (OUTPUT);
BEGIN
 WRITELN ('GOOD MORNING, SUSAN')
END.
```

Note that the word INPUT is not necessary in the program name line because no information is input.

3.

```
PROGRAM CONVERTS (INPUT,OUTPUT);
(*THIS PROGRAM CONVERTS FEET TO METERS*)
VAR
 METERS,FEET : REAL;
BEGIN
 READLN (FEET);
 WRITELN ('LENGTH IN FEET = ',FEET:7:2);
 METERS := FEET/3.281;
 WRITELN ('LENGTH IN METERS = ',METERS:7:2)
END.
```

4.

```
PROGRAM ADDNUMS (INPUT,OUTPUT);
CONST
 INCREASE = 2;
VAR
 NUMBER1,NUMBER2,ANSWER : REAL;
BEGIN
 READLN (NUMBER1,NUMBER2);
 NUMBER1 := NUMBER1 + INCREASE;
 NUMBER2 := NUMBER2 + INCREASE;
 ANSWER := NUMBER1 + NUMBER2;
 WRITELN ('SUM = ', ANSWER:12:3)
END.
```

5.

```
PROGRAM DEBUG (INPUT,OUTPUT);
CONST
 SURCHGE = 15;
VAR
 TOTAL,TAX : REAL;
 PERSONS : INTEGER;
```

```
BEGIN
  READLN (TAX, PERSONS);
  TOTAL := TAX + SURCHGE * PERSONS;
  WRITELN ('THE TOTAL TAX INTAKE IS ', TOTAL:8:2)
END.
```

2

Decision Making Through Control Statements

The main difference between computers and calculators is that computers can compare information and use the comparisons to make decisions. Calculators cannot. This chapter will tell you how to instruct the computer to make decisions.

Simple IF Statements: Decisions Based Upon Whether or Not a Condition Exists

Suppose you find yourself in a situation in which there are two alternatives. You will choose one alternative if a particular condition is true. You will choose the second alternative if a particular condition is false. For example, suppose that you are adding the divorce rates for two cities, RATE1 and RATE2, to find the sum, TOTAL. You want to print the rates and their total, but you want to print the smaller rate first. If RATE1 is smaller, you will print it first. If RATE1 is not smaller, you will print RATE2 first.

You can instruct the computer to compare the rates and carry out an appropriate decision with an IF statement. For example:

```
IF CONDITION-IS-TRUE THEN
  DECISION1
ELSE
  DECISION2;
```

You should represent the condition by an expression and fill in the decision alternatives by appropriate statements. For example:

```
PROGRAM DIVORCE (INPUT,OUTPUT);
(*THIS PROGRAM ADDS 2 RATES & PRINTS THEM ALONG*)
(*WITH THE TOTAL, SMALLEST NUMBER FIRST*)
VAR
  RATE1,RATE2,TOTAL : REAL;
BEGIN
  READLN (RATE1,RATE2);
  TOTAL := RATE1 + RATE2;
  IF RATE1 < RATE2 THEN
    WRITELN (RATE1:8:3,' +',RATE2:8:3,' =',TOTAL:7:3)
  ELSE
    WRITELN (RATE2:8:3,' +',RATE1:8:3,' =',TOTAL:9:3)
END.
```

Note that there is no semicolon after the WRITELN statement that precedes the ELSE part of the IF statement. *Never* put a semicolon before ELSE because the computer will not understand your instructions. There are also no semicolons after THEN or ELSE because the decisions that follow are both part of the same statement.

In the program above, the symbol < (less than) is used to determine if a particular condition (RATE1 < RATE2) is true. The symbol < is called a *relational* operator. If the relationship specified by the relational operator is true, then the condition is true. Otherwise the condition is false. IF statements use the relational operators:

<	less than
>	greater than
=	equal to
<>	not equal to
<=	less than or equal to
>=	greater than or equal to
IN	(see set membership in Chapter 6)

(See the section on Boolean expressions in Chapter 4 for additional *logical* operators that can be used in IF statements.)

You may have a situation in which you want the computer to take an action if a condition is true and to do nothing if a condition is false. In your instruction, omit the ELSE part of the IF statement and specify only one condition and the accompanying decision:

```
IF CONDITION-IS-TRUE THEN
  DECISION;
```

For example, suppose that you want to keep track of the value of 200 shares of a stock and sell them when they are worth at least $4,200. Otherwise, you want to take no action:

```
PROGRAM STOCK (INPUT,OUTPUT);
CONST
  SHARES = 200;
VAR
  STKPRICE,WORTH : REAL;
BEGIN
  READLN (STKPRICE);
  WORTH := SHARES * STKPRICE;
  IF WORTH >= 4200 THEN
    WRITELN ('SELL YOUR STOCK - VALUE = ', WORTH:9:3)
END.
```

Compound Statements Within IF Statements: Decisions Involving Several Statements

In many situations, the decision you want the computer to make, based upon whether or not a condition exists, must be a series of statements, known as *compound statements,* rather than a single statement. A compound statement, like the larger body of your program, starts with the reserved word BEGIN and ends with the reserved word END. If END is followed by ELSE, do not add a semicolon or any other punctuation after END. Otherwise, in a compound statement, END is followed by a semicolon and not by a period, since a period after END signals to the computer the end of the entire program.

For example, another way to find the total of two rates and print the rates and their total, the smaller number first, is to use a compound statement:

```
PROGRAM DIVORCE2 (INPUT,OUTPUT);
VAR
  RATE1,RATE2,HOLD,TOTAL : REAL;
BEGIN
  READLN (RATE1,RATE2);
  TOTAL := RATE1 + RATE2;
  IF RATE1 > RATE2 THEN
    BEGIN
    (*START OF COMPOUND STATEMENT. INDENTED FOR*)
    (*EASE OF READING*)
      HOLD := RATE1;
      RATE1 := RATE2;
      RATE2 := HOLD
    END; (*END OF COMPOUND STATEMENT*)
  WRITELN (RATE1:8:3,' +',RATE2:8:3,' =',TOTAL:9:3)
END.
```

In this program, if RATE1 contains the larger number, then the numbers held in RATE1 and RATE2 are switched in the compound statement so that the smaller number is always placed in RATE1. HOLD is the variable needed to make the switch. It temporarily holds the information in RATE1, since when RATE1 := RATE2 (the information in RATE2 is assigned to RATE1), whatever was previously in RATE1 is lost. Putting that information in HOLD enables you to transfer it to RATE2. If there is no variable in which to hold the RATE1 information temporarily and you have, for example, 50.3 stored in RATE1 and 40.1 stored in RATE2 before the computer switches the information stored in both numbers, the total will be 80.2. You will wind up with the same information in RATE1 and RATE2.

Compound IF Statements: Choosing Among More Than Two Decisions

If you want the computer to distinguish among more than two decisions, you can use a compound IF statement. You type in the decision and expression representing each condition and use the form:

```
IF CONDITION1-IS-TRUE THEN
  DECISION1
ELSE IF CONDITION2-IS-TRUE THEN
  DECISION2
ELSE
  DECISION3;
```

If CONDITION1 and CONDITION2 are both false, the computer will execute DECISION3.

Although the simplest three-decision form is illustrated here, the compound IF statement can instruct the decisions for more than three conditions. The computer will check each condition until it finds one that is true. Then it will execute the decision. Only *one* decision (simple or compound) will be carried out. If all conditions up to the final ELSE are false, it will execute the final decision, since no condition is specified with that ELSE. If you do not include the final ELSE in the IF statement and all specified conditions are false, no decisions will be executed. The final ELSE is usually used when at least one other condition is possible other than the ones you have specified and you want a decision to be carried out if any of these other unspecified conditions are true.

Suppose, for example, that you want the computer to read an average monthly bank account balance. If the bank balance is between zero and $999.99, you want to charge the account $2.50. If the balance is between $1,000 and $2,499.99, you want to post 0.5 percent interest to the account. If the balance is $2,500 or more, you want to post 1.0 percent interest to the account:

```
PROGRAM BANKINT (INPUT,OUTPUT);
CONST
  SAVINT = 0.005;
  (*INTEREST FOR BALANCES BETWEEN $1000 & $2499.99*)
  MMARKINT = 0.01;
  (*INTEREST FOR BALANCES OF $2500 AND OVER*)
VAR
  BALANCE,INTEREST : REAL;
```

```
BEGIN
 READLN (BALANCE);
 IF BALANCE < 0 THEN
  WRITELN ('ERROR - ACCOUNT OVERDRAWN')
 ELSE IF BALANCE < 1000 THEN
  BALANCE := BALANCE - 2.50
 ELSE IF BALANCE < 2500 THEN
  BEGIN
   INTEREST := BALANCE * SAVINT;
   BALANCE := BALANCE + INTEREST
  END (*ELSE-BEGIN*)
 ELSE
  BEGIN
   INTEREST := BALANCE * MMARKINT;
   BALANCE := BALANCE + INTEREST
  END (*ELSE-BEGIN*)
END.
```

Note that the first IF statement in this program is designed to catch the unexpected situation in which an account shows a negative balance. This kind of verification is important if you want to ensure the validity of the input data.

Nested IF Statements: IF Statements Within IF Statements

IF statements become complicated when you want to evaluate another condition once you determine that a condition exists. The general form of nested IF statements is:

```
IF CONDITION1-IS-TRUE THEN
 IF CONDITION2-IS-TRUE THEN
  DECISION1
 ELSE
  DECISION2
ELSE
 DECISION3;
```

When CONDITION1 is evaluated as true, the computer must evaluate whether CONDITION2 is true as well. If both are true, DECISION1 is implemented. If only CONDITION1 is true, DECISION2 is implemented. If CONDITION1 is false, it does not matter that CONDITION2 is true because CONDITION2 is evaluated only if CONDITION1 is true. If CONDITION1 is false, DECISION3 is implemented. The ELSE part of an IF statement will refer to the nearest incomplete IF. IF statements are always nested this way:

```
┌IF
│ ┌IF
│ └ELSE
└ELSE
```

An incorrect nesting would be:

```
┌IF
│ ┌IF
└ELSE
  └ELSE
```

Nested IF statements can create errors in your program that are difficult to find. For example, the preceding nested IF statements provide different instructions than:

```
IF CONDITION1-IS-TRUE THEN
  IF CONDITION2-IS-TRUE THEN
   DECISION1
  ELSE IF CONDITION3-IS-TRUE THEN
   DECISION2
  ELSE
   DECISION3;
```

In these nested IF statements, DECISION3 is implemented only if CONDITION1 is true and CONDITION2 and CONDITION3 are false.

BEGIN and END Statements

The reserved words BEGIN and END delineate compound statements within IF statements. For example, in the next program segment, you want the computer to assign a tax rate of 30 percent to a person whose salary is greater than $25,000; otherwise, the assigned tax rate will be 20 percent. In addition, if a person's salary is greater than $25,000 and he or she has no more than two dependents, you want to impose a surcharge of 10 percent. This is contrasted with a surcharge of 5 percent for more than two dependents and a salary greater than $25,000:

```
IF SALARY > 25000 THEN
  BEGIN
    TAX := 0.3 * SALARY;
    IF NUMDEP <= 2 THEN
      SURCHARG := 0.1 * TAX
    ELSE
      SURCHARG := 0.05 * TAX;
    TAX := TAX + SURCHARG
  END (*IF-BEGIN*)
ELSE TAX := 0.2 * SALARY;
```

The computer will act differently when the same instructions exclude BEGIN and END:

```
IF SALARY > 25000 THEN
  TAX := 0.3 * SALARY;
IF NUMDEP <= 2 THEN
  SURCHARG := 0.1 * TAX
ELSE
  SURCHARG := 0.05 * TAX;
TAX := TAX + SURCHARG
ELSE TAX := 0.2 * SALARY; (*ERROR*)
```

In this segment, the computer will not be able to interpret the instructions, since it appears that there is no incomplete IF statement to which the last ELSE statement can be referred. An error message will result during compilation. In the correct program segment, BEGIN and END are needed to delineate the compound portion of the first IF statement.

CASE Statements: Handling More Than Two Alternatives

You have seen how to use compound IF statements to instruct the computer to choose among more than two alternatives. If it were not possible for you to specify all possible conditions, the final ELSE of the compound IF statement contained a residual decision if all other specified conditions were false.

If it is possible for you to specify all possible conditions, you can also use a CASE statement to instruct the computer to choose among more than two alternatives. Being able to specify all possible conditions is important because if the computer finds no condition specified in the CASE statement that corresponds to the condition it finds in your data, the program will not execute. Instead, you will get an error message.

In a CASE statement, conditions must be specified as *ordinal* values. You can use whole numbers or any other ordinal condition label. *Ordinal* means that your labels are in implicit order. The one appearing first is "less than" the one appearing next, and so on. This is to be distinguished from real numbers, which cannot be used as labels for conditions in CASE statements.

The CASE statement takes the form:

```
CASE VARIABLE-NAME OF
  CONDITION1: DECISION1;
  CONDITION2: DECISION2;
  .
  .
  .
  CONDITION-N: DECISION-N
END;
```

Two or more conditions may be specified. Two or more conditions may also lead to the same decision, for example:

```
CASE VARIABLE-NAME OF
  CONDITION1,CONDITION2: DECISION1;
  CONDITION3: DECISION2;
  CONDITION4: DECISION3:
END;
```

A decision can also be a compound statement delineated by the reserved words BEGIN and END. For example:

```
CASE VARIABLE-NAME OF
 CONDITION1:
  BEGIN (*DECISION1*)
   STATEMENT1;
   STATEMENT2
  END; (*DECISION1*)
 CONDITION2: DECISION2;
 CONDITION3: DECISION3
END;
```

If a particular condition is found and you want no action taken, leave out the decision statement:

```
CASE VARIABLE-NAME OF
 CONDITION1: ;
 CONDITION2: DECISION
END;
```

To take no action if a particular condition is found and that condition is the last case delineated, omit the semicolon after CONDITION: because the reserved word END follows.

Let's look at several of these forms in actual Pascal instructions.

```
CASE ROMANCVT OF
(*ROMANCVT IS THE VARIABLE-NAME HERE*)
 'I': ARABNUM := 1;
 'V': ARABNUM := 5;
 'X': ARABNUM := 10;
 'L': ARABNUM := 50;
 'C': ARABNUM := 100;
 'D': ARABNUM := 500;
 'M': ARABNUM := 1000
END;
```

The CASE statement above converts Roman numerals into their Arabic equivalents. If the condition 'V' is encountered, for example, the variable ARABNUM is assigned a value of five.

The next program is based upon PROGRAM BANKINT earlier in the chapter. Here, an account is assigned an ordinal value, depending upon its average monthly balance. Interest is then posted or a bank account charged, according to the average monthly bank balance, in the CASE statement:

```
PROGRAM BANKINT (INPUT,OUTPUT);
VAR
  BALANCE,INTEREST,SAVINT : REAL;
  BANK : INTEGER;
BEGIN
  SAVINT := 0.01;
  READLN (BALANCE);
  IF BALANCE < 0 THEN
    WRITELN ('ERROR - ACCOUNT OVERDRAWN')
  ELSE
    BEGIN
    IF BALANCE < 1000 THEN
      BANK := 1
    ELSE IF BALANCE < 2500 THEN
      BEGIN
        BANK := 2;
        SAVINT := 0.005
      END (*ELSE-BEGIN*)
    ELSE
      BANK := 3;
    CASE BANK OF
      1:  BALANCE := BALANCE - 2.50;
      2,3:
          BEGIN
            INTEREST := BALANCE * SAVINT;
            BALANCE := BALANCE + INTEREST
          END
    END (*CASE*)
    END (*ELSE-BEGIN*)
END.
```

Review Exercises

1. Write a program to read the population of three different countries and to print the largest figure.

2. Workers in a factory receive a bonus of $25 if they produce over their quota of 200 items per week. In addition, they get an additional 50 percent of their hourly rate for any hours over forty that they work per week. Write a program to com-

pute and print a worker's salary for the week according to number of hours worked, hourly rate and whether or not a bonus is due.

3. Sale items in a store are marked at 20 percent (yellow tag), 30 percent (green tag), and 40 percent (red tag) off list price, depending upon whether the list price of the item is $20 or less, $20.01 to $100, or over $100, respectively. Write a program to determine the sale price of an item and to print next to an item's stock number its sale price. Also determine whether it is a yellow-tag, green-tag, or red-tag item.

4. Write a program that prints both a patient's cholesterol level and a message if the cholesterol level exceeds the following limits for different age groups:

AGE	LEVEL (MG/DL)
1-29	240
30-39	270
40-49	310
50 or over	330

5. Write a program to determine the volume of a candy container, depending upon whether it is a right circular cone ($V = 1/3\pi r^2 h$), a right circular cylinder ($V = \pi r^2 h$), or a sphere ($V = 4/3\pi r^3$).

Answers to Review Exercises

1.

```
PROGRAM LARGEST (INPUT,OUTPUT);
VAR
 POP1,POP2,POP3,LARGE : INTEGER;
BEGIN
 READLN (POP1,POP2,POP3);
 IF POP2 > POP1 THEN
  LARGE := POP2
  ELSE LARGE := POP1;
 IF POP3 > LARGE THEN
  LARGE := POP3;
 WRITELN ('THE LARGEST NUMBER IS', LARGE :12)
END.
```

2.

```
PROGRAM FACTORY (INPUT,OUTPUT);
CONST
  BONUS = 25;
VAR
  WORKNUM,QUOT : INTEGER;
  (*WORKNUM IS THE NUMBER OF THE WORKER*)
  (*QUOT IS ITEMS PRODUCED THIS WEEK *)
  HRWAGE,HRSWORK,SALARY : REAL;
  (*HRWAGE IS HOURLY WAGE OF THE WORKER*)
  (*HRSWORK IS HOURS WORKED THIS WEEK*)
  (*SALARY IS SALARY THIS WEEK*)
BEGIN
  READLN (WORKNUM,QUOT,HRWAGE,HRSWORK);
  IF HRSWORK > 40 THEN
    SALARY := 40*HRWAGE+(HRSWORK-40)*HRWAGE*1.5
  ELSE
    SALARY := HRSWORK * HRWAGE;
  IF QUOT > 200 THEN
    SALARY := SALARY + BONUS;
  WRITELN (WORKNUM:5,SALARY:8:2)
END.
```

3.

```
PROGRAM STORESAL (INPUT,OUTPUT);
VAR
  LISTPRCE,SALEPRCE : REAL;
  STOCKNUM : INTEGER;
BEGIN
  READLN (STOCKNUM,LISTPRCE);
  WRITE (STOCKNUM:10);
  IF LISTPRCE <= 20 THEN
    BEGIN
      SALEPRCE := LISTPRCE * 0.80;
      WRITELN (SALEPRCE:8:2,' YELLOW TAG')
    END (*IF-BEGIN*)
  ELSE IF LISTPRCE <= 100 THEN
    BEGIN
      SALEPRCE := LISTPRCE * 0.70;
      WRITELN (SALEPRCE:8:2,' GREEN TAG')
    END (*ELSE-BEGIN*)
  ELSE
    BEGIN
      SALEPRCE := LISTPRCE * 0.60;
      WRITELN (SALEPRCE:8:2,' RED TAG')
    END (*ELSE-BEGIN*)
END.
```

4.

```
PROGRAM CHOLEST (INPUT,OUTPUT);
VAR
 CLEVEL,AGE : INTEGER;
BEGIN
 READLN (CLEVEL,AGE);
 WRITE ('CHOLESTEROL LEVEL IS:',CLEVEL:5);
 IF AGE <= 29 THEN
  BEGIN
   IF CLEVEL > 240 THEN
    WRITELN (' LEVEL EXCEEDS NORMAL LIMITS')
   END (*IF-BEGIN*)
 ELSE IF AGE <= 39 THEN
  BEGIN
   IF CLEVEL > 270 THEN
    WRITELN (' LEVEL EXCEEDS NORMAL LIMITS')
   END (*ELSE-BEGIN*)
 ELSE IF AGE <= 49 THEN
  BEGIN
   IF CLEVEL > 310 THEN
    WRITELN (' LEVEL EXCEEDS NORMAL LIMITS')
   END (*ELSE-BEGIN*)
 ELSE
  IF CLEVEL > 330 THEN
   WRITELN (' LEVEL EXCEEDS NORMAL LIMITS');
 WRITELN
END.
```

5.

```
PROGRAM VOLUME (INPUT,OUTPUT);
CONST
 PI = 3.1416;
VAR
 SHAPE : INTEGER;
 (*1=RIGHT CIRCULAR CONE, 2=RIGHT CIRCULAR*)
 (*CYLINDER, 3=SPHERE*)
 VOLUME,RADIUS,HEIGHT : REAL;
BEGIN
 READ (SHAPE,RADIUS);
 CASE SHAPE OF
  1:
   BEGIN
    READLN (HEIGHT);
    VOLUME := PI * RADIUS * RADIUS * HEIGHT/3
   END;
```

```
    2:
     BEGIN
      READLN (HEIGHT);
      VOLUME := PI * RADIUS * RADIUS * HEIGHT
     END;
    3: VOLUME := 4 * PI * RADIUS * RADIUS * RADIUS/3
  END; (*CASE*)
  WRITELN ('VOLUME=', VOLUME:10:4)
END.
```

3

Loops and Repetitive Tasks

One major value of a computer is that it performs repetitive computations quickly, particularly when you have more than one computation that must be performed several times. This is generally done by means of some kind of loop.

WHILE Loops: Getting the Computer to Perform Repetitive Tasks

WHILE loops instruct the computer to perform one or more actions, so long as a particular condition holds. They take the form:

```
WHILE CONDITION-IS-TRUE DO
  STATEMENT;
```

The condition is represented by an expression. The statement in a WHILE loop may be single or compound, in which case it is bordered by the reserved words BEGIN and END. Usually, WHILE loops contain compound statements because there is often a counter in the loop that updates a variable in the expression that represents the condition and at least one other statement containing instructions for the repetitive task. For example:

```
PROGRAM CONVERT (OUTPUT);
VAR
  KILO : REAL;
  MILE : INTEGER;
BEGIN
  MILE := 0; (*initialize*)
  WHILE MILE < 50 DO
    BEGIN
      MILE := MILE + 1; (*COUNTER*)
      KILO := MILE * 1.6094;
      WRITELN (MILE:4,KILO:18:4)
    END
END.
```

The program above converts miles from 1 to 50 into kilometers. MILE is first *initialized* to zero. Initialization defines a variables's starting value. Whenever you use WHILE loops, always initialize the variable that you will use as a counter and do this *outside* of the WHILE loop. In this program, MILE is the counter. Then, when the variable is evaluated at the beginning of the WHILE loop, it has a specified value. This way, the computer will be able to evaluate whether or not the condition defined in the WHILE loop is true. This evaluation determines whether the computer enters the loop the first time; later evaluations determine whether or not the loop will be reentered.

Before the first encounter of the WHILE loop, MILE has been assigned a value of zero. Since MILE is less than 50, the computer enters the loop. MILE is increased by 1, so its value is now 1, printing "1.6094" as the corresponding kilometer value. Since MILE is still less than 50, the loop is reentered. MILE is incremented again, so it now equals 2, printing "3.2188" kilometers. This continues until MILE is incremented to 50, printing "80.4700" kilometers. At this point, it is time to evaluate again the condition specified in the WHILE statement. MILE < 50, the condition for reentering the loop, no longer holds, so the program continues with the statement after the WHILE loop. In this case, it brings you to the end of the program.

Let's look at another example of a WHILE loop, based upon the tax program in Chapter 2. It instructs the computer to read a series of workers' salaries and to continue to read salaries and compute taxes until NEXT—a counter for the number of workers being evaluated here—is a number equal to NUMWKERS. NUMWKERS can be defined as a constant in your constant declaration, equal to the number of workers on whom you have information.

You can also use a marker value here to ensure that all items of information have been read in to be processed. This is a value that would not ordinarily occur. For example, if there are 100 workers, each with a worker number, WORKNUM, between 1 and 100, you can use a value of 999 as a final value in your input file. You would then instruct the computer to read the next WORKNUM at the end of the loop. Your WHILE condition statement might then read WHILE WORK-NUM <> 999 DO. When 999 was encountered in your data file, the loop would be terminated.

```
NEXT := 0; (*COUNTER FOR NUMBER OF WORKERS*)
WHILE NEXT < NUMWKERS DO
  BEGIN
    NEXT := NEXT + 1; (*INCREMENT COUNTER*)
    READ (SALARY);
    IF SALARY > 25000 THEN
      BEGIN
        TAX := 0.3 * SALARY;
        IF NUMDEP <= 2 THEN
          SURCHARG := 0.1 * TAX
        ELSE
          SURCHARG := 0.05 * TAX;
        TAX := TAX + SURCHARG
      END (*IF-BEGIN*)
    ELSE
      TAX := 0.2 * SALARY;
    WRITELN (' SALARY=',SALARY:10:2,'TAX=',TAX:8:2)
  END; (*WHILE-BEGIN*)
```

Let's look at an example of a WHILE loop that does not contain a counter; instead, it controls the operation of the loop by means of whether or not a built-in *function*—EOF (end of data file)—is a condition that is true. A function executes a particular task and returns a value, in this case determining whether or not there is more data in the file. This program segment copies line for line as output whatever integers (the variable TEXTNUM here) are input:

```
WHILE NOT EOF DO
  BEGIN
    READ (TEXTNUM);
    WRITE (TEXTNUM);
    IF EOLN THEN
      BEGIN
        READLN;
        WRITELN
      END (*IF-BEGIN*)
  END; (*WHILE-BEGIN*)
```

Another built-in function, EOLN (end of line), is used in the IF statement. When the end of a line of data is reached, the computer moves to the next line. (More built-in functions can be found in Chapter 5.)

FOR Loops:
A Second Way to Repeat Execution

FOR loops instruct the computer to perform one or more actions while an index value increments or decrements in steps of one from a specified start value to a specified finish value.

To count from a smaller start value to a larger end value, use the form:

```
FOR INDEX-CONTROL-VARIABLE := START TO FINISH DO
  STATEMENT;
```

To count down from a larger start value to a smaller end value, use the form:

```
FOR INDEX-CONTROL-VARIABLE := START DOWNTO FINISH DO
STATEMENT;
```

In various forms of counting, FOR loops are more concise than WHILE loops. If you know beforehand how many passes will be made through the loop (how many repetitions will be made), use a FOR loop. For example:

```
PROGRAM SQUARES (OUTPUT);
VAR
  NUMBER,SQUARE : INTEGER;
BEGIN
  FOR NUMBER := 1 TO 100 DO
    BEGIN
      SQUARE := NUMBER * NUMBER;
      WRITELN (NUMBER:4,SQUARE:9)
    END (*FOR-BEGIN*)
END.
```

This program prints a list of the numbers and their squares from 1 to 100. To do the same thing using a WHILE loop, you would first have to initialize NUMBERS and include a counter in the WHILE loop statement to update NUMBERS:

```
PROGRAM SQUARES (OUTPUT);
VAR
  NUMBER,SQUARE : INTEGER;
BEGIN
  NUMBER := 0;
  WHILE NUMBER < 100 DO
    BEGIN
      NUMBER := NUMBER + 1;
      SQUARE := NUMBER * NUMBER;
      WRITELN (NUMBER:4,SQUARE:6)
    END (*WHILE-BEGIN*)
END.
```

A FOR loop may contain compound statements, as in PROGRAM SQUARES above, or as in the program:

```
PROGRAM ADDMULT (OUTPUT);
VAR
  SUM,PROD,I : INTEGER;
BEGIN
  SUM := 0; (*INITIALIZE*)
  FOR I := 1 TO 5 DO
    BEGIN
      SUM := SUM + I;
      PROD := SUM * I;
      WRITELN (SUM:3,PROD:6)
    END (*FOR-BEGIN*)
END.
```

Pause here and try to write the output. Then examine and make sure that you understand why the output looks this way:

```
 1       1
 3       6
 6      18
10      40
15      75
```

When creating FOR loops, five additional rules apply:

1. The index control variable that you select may be of any data type discussed so far (or of those discussed in Chapter 4 under standard or enumerated type), except *real*.

2. The index control variable must be of the same type as the START and FINISH values that you specify in the FOR statement.

3. The START and FINISH values may be constants, variables or more complex expressions, such as:

FOR INDEX : = 1 TO COUNT−1 DO

4. The value of the index control variable should not be changed once you are inside the loop, since the loop itself automatically increments or decrements it.

5. Once you exit the FOR loop, the index control variable no longer has a defined value.

REPEAT . . . UNTIL Loops:
A Third Way to Repeat Execution

REPEAT . . . UNTIL loops instruct the computer to perform one or more actions until a specified condition is true. Unlike WHILE loops, which may never be entered if the condition specified in the WHILE loop is not true, REPEAT . . . UNTIL loops are always entered at least once. This occurs because the condition that terminates the loop is not examined to see if it is true until the end of one pass through the loop. If the condition is true, the computer will leave the loop and execute the statement following the loop. REPEAT . . . UNTIL loops take the form:

```
REPEAT
  STATEMENT
UNTIL CONDITION;
```

Although the statement in the REPEAT . . . UNTIL loop may be a compound statement, you do not have to use the reserved words BEGIN and END around the compound statement.

The next program is a variation of PROGRAM SQUARES, which you have seen in this chapter in both a WHILE loop version and a FOR loop version. Here is the REPEAT . . . UNTIL loop version:

```
PROGRAM SQUARES (OUTPUT);
VAR
  NUMBER,SQUARE : INTEGER;
BEGIN
  NUMBER := 0;
  REPEAT
    NUMBER := NUMBER + 1;
    SQUARE := NUMBER * NUMBER;
    WRITELN (NUMBER:4,SQUARE:6)
  UNTIL NUMBER = 100
END.
```

Note that in the WHILE LOOP version, the loop was entered while the condition specified was true. In contrast, in the REPEAT . . . UNTIL loop version, the loop is executed while the condition specified is false, and the loop is exited once it is true.

Let's look at one additional program segment that uses a REPEAT . . . UNTIL loop. This program segment searches a field of grades for those that are less than sixty and flags them as failing grades:

```
REPEAT
  READLN (STUDENUM,GRADE);
  WRITE (STUDENUM:11,GRADE:5);
  IF GRADE < 60 THEN
    WRITELN (' FAILING GRADE')
  ELSE
    WRITELN
UNTIL EOF;
```

GOTO Statements: Creating or Exiting a Loop

A GOTO statement refers the computer to a place in the program block marked by a label. The label you select must be an unsigned integer with a maximum of four digits followed by a colon. The form of a GOTO statement is:

```
GOTO LABEL-NUMBER;
```

The form of a label is:

```
LABEL-NUMBER : STATEMENT;
```

Labels must be declared before constants and variables:

```
LABEL
 LABEL-NUMBER1 , LABEL-NUMBER2;
```

Each label can be used for only one statement in the program block.

GOTO statements can be used to simulate the actions of WHILE, FOR, and REPEAT . . . UNTIL loops. For example,

```
WHILE CONDITION DO
 STATEMENT;
NEXT-STATEMENT;
```

becomes:

```
10 : IF NOT-CONDITION THEN
       GOTO 99;
     STATEMENT;
     GOTO 10;
99 : NEXT-STATEMENT;
```

In general, avoid using GOTO statements, since they often make a program difficult to read. They can, however, be used for the orderly termination of a loop from within the loop. For example:

```
      FOR I := 1 TO 100 DO
        BEGIN
          STATEMENT;
          IF CONDITION THEN
            GOTO 20
        END; (*FOR-BEGIN*)
20 : WRITELN (' CONDITIONAL LOOP EXIT');
```

Nested Loops :
For More Complex Repetition of Tasks

Program segments may contain two or more loops nested within one another. For example, the next program has both an inner and outer FOR loop. The entire inner loop is executed for each of the index control values of the outer loop. Since the outer loop is repeated four times, the inner loop is executed for JINDEX values 1 to 5 for each of the four index values of the outer loop.

```
FOR INDEX := 1 to 4 DO
  BEGIN
    WRITELN (' INDEX=',INDEX:2);
    FOR JINDEX := 1 TO 5 DO
      WRITELN ('        JINDEX=',JINDEX:2)
  END; (*FOR-BEGIN*)
```

The output will look like this:

```
INDEX= 1
        JINDEX= 1
        JINDEX= 2
        JINDEX= 3
        JINDEX= 4
        JINDEX= 5
INDEX= 2
        JINDEX= 1
        JINDEX= 2
        JINDEX= 3
        JINDEX= 4
        JINDEX= 5
INDEX= 3
        JINDEX= 1
        JINDEX= 2
        JINDEX= 3
        JINDEX= 4
        JINDEX= 5
INDEX= 4
        JINDEX= 1
        JINDEX= 2
        JINDEX= 3
        JINDEX= 4
        JINDEX= 5
```

The next program segment demonstrates the use of EOF (end of file) and EOLN (end of line) in nested loops. Another program segment using these two built-in functions was presented earlier in the chapter under WHILE loops:

```
REPEAT
  WHILE NOT EOLN DO
    BEGIN
      READ (IDNUM,TEMP);
      IF TEMP < 32 THEN
        WRITELN (IDNUM:6,TEMP:8:2)
    END; (*WHILE-BEGIN*)
    READLN
UNTIL EOF;
```

This program segment tells the computer to read pairs of identification numbers and temperatures in a file and to list those that are subfreezing. At the end of a line in the file, it instructs the computer to skip to the next line and continue to the end of the file.

Review Exercises

1.   A factorial is the product of a positive integer multiplied by all positive integers less than it. For example, three factorial is $3 \times 2 \times 1 = 6$. Write a program to compute and print the factorial of a number.

2.   Write a program to compute and print the mean of a list of selling prices for homes.

3.   Write a program using a GOTO statement to read and print an input file of single digit numbers, representing scores on a happiness scale, and to stop when a number with more than one digit is encountered.

4.   Write a program that reads the homicide rates per capita for a list of cities and prints the minimum and maximum rates.

5.   Modify the program segment on page 38, which copies line for line whatever integers are input. Change it so that the number of lines specified in the constant NUMLINES is skipped between each line of integers being printed.

Answers to Review Exercises

1.
```
PROGRAM FACT (INPUT,OUTPUT);
VAR
 PRODUCT,INDEX,NUMBER : INTEGER;
BEGIN
 READLN (NUMBER);
 PRODUCT := 1; (*INITIALIZE*)
 FOR INDEX := 1 TO NUMBER DO
   PRODUCT := PRODUCT * INDEX;
 WRITELN (NUMBER:6,' FACTORIAL =',PRODUCT:8)
END.
```

Another version, using a WHILE loop:

```
PROGRAM FACT (INPUT,OUTPUT);
VAR
 PRODUCT,NUMBER : INTEGER;
BEGIN
 READLN (NUMBER);
 WRITE (NUMBER:6,'  FACTORIAL =');
 PRODUCT := 1;
 WHILE NUMBER <> 0 DO
   BEGIN
     PRODUCT := NUMBER * PRODUCT;
     NUMBER := NUMBER - 1
   END; (*WHILE-BEGIN*)
 WRITELN (PRODUCT:8)
END.
```

2.
```
PROGRAM AVERAGE (INPUT,OUTPUT);
VAR
 COUNT : INTEGER;
 MEAN,SUM,PRICE : REAL;
BEGIN
 COUNT := 0;
 SUM := 0;
 REPEAT
   READLN (PRICE);
   SUM := SUM + PRICE;
   COUNT := COUNT + 1
 UNTIL EOF;
 MEAN := SUM/COUNT;
 WRITELN ('THE MEAN IS',MEAN:12:2)
END.
```

3.

```
PROGRAM PROOF (INPUT,OUTPUT);
LABEL
 1;
VAR
 HAPPI : INTEGER;
BEGIN
 WHILE NOT EOF DO
  BEGIN
   READ (HAPPI);
   WRITE (HAPPI);
   IF HAPPI > 9 THEN GOTO 1;
   IF EOLN THEN
    BEGIN
     READLN;
     WRITELN
    END (*IF-BEGIN*)
  END; (*WHILE-BEGIN*)
1: END.
```

4.

```
PROGRAM MINMAX (INPUT,OUTPUT);
VAR
 MINIMUM,MAXIMUM,HOMICIDE : REAL;
BEGIN
 READLN (HOMICIDE);
 MINIMUM := HOMICIDE;
 MAXIMUM := HOMICIDE;
 WHILE NOT EOF DO
  BEGIN
   READLN (HOMICIDE);
   IF HOMICIDE < MINIMUM THEN
    MINIMUM := HOMICIDE
   ELSE IF HOMICIDE > MAXIMUM THEN
    MAXIMUM := HOMICIDE
  END; (*WHILE-BEGIN*)
 WRITELN ('THE MINIMUM =',MINIMUM:9:2);
 WRITELN ('THE MAXIMUM =',MAXIMUM:9:2)
END.
```

5.

```
WHILE NOT EOF DO
  BEGIN
    READ (TEXTNUM);
    WRITE (TEXTNUM);
    IF EOLN THEN
      BEGIN
      FOR I := 1 TO NUMLINES + 1 DO
        WRITELN;
      READLN
      END (*IF-BEGIN*)
  END; (*WHILE-BEGIN*)
```

4

Char and Boolean Data Types and Additional Type Declarations

Variable declarations were illustrated in the programs in the first three chapters, and Chapter 1 introduced two standard data types—integer and real. In this chapter, the data types char and Boolean will be introduced. Subrange and enumerated type declarations also will be described.

CHAR: A Data Type for Characters

Chapter 3 contains a program segment used to demonstrate WHILE loops that copies line for line as output whatever integers are input. The variable that contains each file value is called TEXTNUM in this program segment. If the input file had been composed of letters of the alphabet or of a combination of letters and numbers, a declaration of real or integer for the variable would not be adequate to describe its type because it would not always contain a number. Instead, you would be working with a variable that contains a *character*. Characters include letters of the alphabet as well as punctuation marks, blanks, and digits. If digits are treated as characters and not as numbers, they can be read, compared, and printed, but they cannot be manipulated arithmetically.

A variable that contains a character value is of char type. A character value of char type can be only a single character, and it is enclosed in single quotes in declarations and statements. For example:

```
PROGRAM DEMO;
CONST
  BLANK = ' ';
VAR
  TEXTCHAR : CHAR;
BEGIN
  TEXTCHAR := 'A';
  .
  .
  .
END.
```

Character variables can be compared using the relational operators:

```
<
>
=
<>
<=
>=
```
IN (also see set membership in Chapter 6)

For example, to increment the counter ACOUNT when A is encountered and keep track of the number of A characters in your input:

```
IF SYMBOL = 'A' THEN
  ACOUNT := ACOUNT + 1;
```

Char values are also compared through a set of ordinal numbers that represent the character set. These ordinal numbers vary from system to system, but they can be determined and worked with using the built-in function ORD. ORD ('A'), for example, reveals the value of the ordinal number of the character A. With most systems, ORD ('A') is one less than ORD ('B'), etc. For example, to use ORD in a program statement with the char variable SYM:

```
IF (ORD(SYM) >= ORD('0')) AND (ORD(SYM) <= ORD('9')) THEN
  WRITELN (' CHARACTER IS A NUMBER BETWEEN 0 AND 9');
```

This program segment prints out a message if the computer encounters a digit between zero and 9. Computer systems vary in the character sets that can be used and whether lowercase, uppercase or both forms of alphabetic characters are acceptable char values.

If you want to know the character that corresponds to a particular ordinal number, the built-in function CHR will return this value. The form for calling the function is:

```
CHR (INTEGER-EXPRESSION)
```

Remember that the integer expression you specify may consist of a single integer value.

PRED and SUCC are two additional built-in functions that can be used in program statements. PRED ('A'), for example, returns the character with the ordinal number *preceding* A. SUCC ('9') returns the character with the next largest ordinal number after that corresponding to the character 9.

The next program is an example of the declaration and use of a char variable. It prints the text and counts the number of periods in the text:

```
PROGRAM PERIODS (INPUT,OUTPUT);
CONST
  TERMNATE = '$';
  (*A MARKER VALUE THAT SIGNALS THE END OF THE TEXT*)
VAR
  NEXTCHAR : CHAR;
  PERCOUNT : INTEGER;
  (*COUNT OF THE NUMBER OF PERIODS*)
BEGIN
  PERCOUNT := 0; (*INITIALIZE*)
  WRITE (' THE TEXT IS ');
  READ (NEXTCHAR);
  WHILE NEXTCHAR <> TERMNATE DO
    BEGIN
      WRITE (NEXTCHAR);
      IF NEXTCHAR = '.' THEN
        PERCOUNT := PERCOUNT + 1;
```

```
    IF EOLN THEN
      BEGIN
        READLN;
        WRITELN
      END; (*IF-BEGIN*)
     READ (NEXTCHAR)
   END; (*WHILE-BEGIN*)
  WRITELN;
  WRITELN (' THE NUMBER OF PERIODS IS: ',PERCOUNT:4)
END.
```

BOOLEAN:
A Data Type for True or False Values

Let's return to the program segment in Chapter 3 that uses the built-in functions EOF and EOLN to demonstrate WHILE loops. If the condition NOT EOF is true, then the WHILE loop is entered. If the end of the file is not yet reached, NOT EOF is true. Similarly, whether EOLN is true determines whether the compound statement in the IF statement is executed. When the end of a line is reached, EOLN is true. These are examples of Boolean functions. Variables (as well as constants) that you declare in your program can also be of Boolean type. This means that the data in the variable must be either the value true or the value false. For example:

```
PROGRAM ALPHABET (OUTPUT);
VAR
  ALPH : CHAR;
  MARKER : BOOLEAN;
BEGIN
  ALPH := 'A';
  MARKER := FALSE;
  WHILE NOT MARKER DO
    BEGIN
      WRITE (ALPH:3);
      ALPH := SUCC (ALPH);
      IF PRED (ALPH) = 'Z' THEN
        MARKER := TRUE
    END (*WHILE-BEGIN*)
END.
```

The program above prints the letters of the alphabet from A to Z and uses the Boolean variable MARKER to determine when the characters have gone beyond the uppercase letters of the alphabet. This terminates the WHILE loop. WHILE NOT MARKER DO could also have been written as WHILE MARKER = FALSE.

Boolean expressions are often more complex than this. OR, as well as AND, can be used to form more complicated expressions. With OR, if either expression is true, the value returned is true. With AND, both expressions must be true for the value of true to be returned. NOT, AND, and OR are the order of precedence in which these logical operators are applied.

Precedence Order

```
NOT
*, /, DIV, MOD, AND
+, -, OR
<, >, =, <>, <=, >=
```

To make your entire expression clear, you might want to use parentheses. The following are all valid Boolean expressions (I,J,K, and L are of integer type; MARKER is of Boolean type):

```
NOT MARKER OR ((I + J) <= (K + L))
(I < 3) AND (J > 10)
(I >= 10) OR (K = L)
(I > J) AND (NOT MARKER)
```

All the relational operators you have seen can be used in creating Boolean expressions. Most of the built-in functions you have seen so far—EOF, EOLN, PRED, SUCC, ORD—and an additional built-in function, ODD, can also be useful. For example, ODD (X) yields a value of true if the value in variable X is odd and a value of false if it is even. You can use any integer variable or expression within the parentheses.

The next program computes and lists all prime numbers between 50 and 100. PRIME is a Boolean variable that is initialized to true outside of the inner FOR loop. If a number has a divisor other than 1 and itself—MOD division results in a zero—then that number is not a prime number and PRIME is assigned a value of false. If PRIME is true at the termination of the inner loop, the number is listed as a prime number:

```
PROGRAM PRIMENUM (OUTPUT);
VAR
 I,DIVISOR : INTEGER;
 PRIME : BOOLEAN;
BEGIN
 FOR I := 50 TO 100 DO
   BEGIN
     PRIME := TRUE;
     FOR DIVISOR := 2 TO I - 1 DO
      IF (I MOD DIVISOR) = 0 THEN
        PRIME := FALSE;
     IF PRIME THEN
       WRITELN (I:6)
   END (*FOR-BEGIN*)
END.
```

Subrange Type Declarations: Specifying Minimum and Maximum Values

You have now seen how to use the data types integer, real, char, and Boolean in variable declarations. TYPE declarations can be inserted between CONST and VAR declarations if you want to describe further the values that a variable will have.

If you know that a variable will have values within an ordinal range, you should declare this range. Then if the computer encounters a value outside of the specified range, it will inform you. This is a useful way to catch errors in inputting data or mistakes in your instructions.

The form for declaring a subrange type is:

TYPE_NAME = MIN-VALUE..MAX-VALUE;

For example, if you are reading in a list of exam scores, all of which vary from zero to 100, you can declare the bounds as:

```
TYPE
  SCORES = 0..100;
VAR
  EXAM : SCORES;
```

MIN-VALUE and/or MAX-VALUE may be constants. For example:

```
CONST
  MAX = 100;
TYPE
  SCORES = 0..MAX;
VAR
  EXAM : SCORES;
```

Note how the type declaration also changes the variable declaration. EXAM is no longer explicitly integer. It is of type SCORES, which you have declared in the TYPE section. But since SCORES, or the subrange zero to 100, is implicitly a subrange of integer type, any of the operators or processes that can be done on integer data can be done on the values in the variable EXAM. Note also that your type name—SCORES in this case—must be a valid identifier.

Enumerated Type Declarations: Specifying All Possible Values

If you know that a variable will have only a limited set of values, you can declare this set of values. Like subrange type declarations, this is a useful way to catch errors.

The form for declaring an enumerated type is:

<u>TYPE-NAME</u> = (<u>LIST OF VALUES</u>);

For example, the list of values associated with days of the week can be represented as:

```
TYPE
  DAY = (SUN,MON,TUES,WEDS,THUR,FRI,SAT);
VAR
  DAYWEEK : DAY;
```

You can also use enumerated types in a subrange. For example:

```
TYPE
  DAY = (SUN,MON,TUES,WEDS,THURS,FRI,SAT);
  WEEKDAY = MON..FRI;
VAR
  D : DAY ;
  WORKDAY : WEEKDAY;
```

The values in the subrange, however, must be listed in order in the enumerated type declaration. You cannot, for example, declare WEEKEND = SAT..SUN; because SAT and SUN do not follow each other in the declaration here. You also cannot use the same value name in two enumerated type declarations. WEEKEND = (SAT,SUN) would not be correct if SAT and SUN already appeared in the enumerated type DAY. An enumerated type value should appear in *only one* enumerated type declaration. Each value should be a valid identifier.

Although enumerated type values make a program easier to follow, the computer reads and prints numbers corresponding to the enumerated type values. For example, if you wanted the computer to print a day of the week corresponding to a particular date, you might use:

```
PROGRAM CALENDAR (INPUT,OUTPUT);
 .
 .
 .
VAR
  DAYWEEK : DAY;
 .
 .
 .
CASE DAYWEEK OF
  SUNDAY   : WRITELN ('SUNDAY');
  MONDAY   : WRITELN ('MONDAY');
  TUESDAY  : WRITELN ('TUESDAY');
  WEDNESDAY : WRITELN ('WEDNESDAY');
  THURSDAY : WRITELN ('THURSDAY');
  FRIDAY   : WRITELN ('FRIDAY');
  SATURDAY : WRITELN ('SATURDAY')
```

```
END;
  .
  .
  .
```

You would need a similar CASE statement earlier in the program, setting each of the enumerated type values to an input number, since the enumerated type values cannot be read directly. For example:

```
1 : DAYWEEK := SUNDAY;
2 : DAYWEEK := MONDAY;
```

Review Exercises

1. You must write an essay that is no longer than 300 sentences. Write a program that counts the number of sentences by counting the number of periods followed by a blank space.

2. You want to send a message in code to your business partner. Write a program that creates a code for each word in a list by replacing each letter with the letter following it in the alphabet. Have Z replaced by A. Assume that all letters used are uppercase.

3. Your friend is embarrassed to tell your how much she weighs and will do so only in cryptic form. Write a program that reads a line of characters and converts any digits in the line to numeric values. The program should print the sum of all the digits (your friend's weight).

4. The arithmetic operators $+$, $-$, $*$, and $/$ can be used with either integer or real numbers. These operators have an order of precedence in that without parentheses, multiplication and division are performed before addition and subtraction. Write a program that reads and prints two operators and determines and prints which has precedence.

Answers to Review Exercises

1.

```
PROGRAM SENTENCE (INPUT,OUTPUT);
CONST
  BLANK = ' ';
VAR
  NEXT : CHAR;
  SENTCNT : INTEGER;
  (*COUNTS THE NUMBER OF SENTENCES*)
BEGIN
  SENTCNT := 0; (*INITIALIZE*)
  READ (NEXT);
  WHILE NOT EOF DO
    BEGIN
      IF NEXT = '.' THEN
        BEGIN
          READ (NEXT);
          IF (NEXT = BLANK) OR (EOF) OR (EOLN) THEN
            SENTCNT := SENTCNT + 1
        END; (*IF-BEGIN*)
      READ (NEXT);
      IF EOLN THEN
        READLN
    END; (*WHILE-BEGIN*)
  WRITELN (' THE NUMBER OF SENTENCES IS',SENTCNT:5)
END.
```

2.

```
PROGRAM CODELETR (INPUT,OUTPUT);
TYPE
  ALPH = 'A'..'Z';
VAR
  CHTR : ALPH;
BEGIN
  READ (CHTR);
  WHILE NOT EOF DO
    BEGIN
      IF CHTR = 'Z' THEN
        CHTR := 'A'
      ELSE
        IF CHTR IN ['A'..'Z'] THEN
          CHTR := SUCC (CHTR);
      WRITE (CHTR);
      IF EOLN THEN
```

```
        BEGIN
         READLN;
         WRITELN
        END; (*IF-BEGIN*)
      READ (CHTR)
    END (*WHILE-BEGIN*)
  END.
```

3.
```
  PROGRAM CRYPTIC (INPUT,OUTPUT);
  VAR
   CHTR : CHAR;
   DIGIT,SUM : INTEGER;
  BEGIN
   SUM := 0;
   READ (CHTR);
   WHILE NOT EOLN DO
     BEGIN
       IF (ORD(CHTR) >= ORD('0')) AND
         (ORD(CHTR) <= ORD('9')) THEN
         BEGIN
           DIGIT := (ORD(CHTR)-ORD('0'));
           SUM := SUM + DIGIT
         END; (*IF-BEGIN*)
       READ (CHTR)
     END; (*WHILE-BEGIN*)
   WRITELN ('WEIGHT =',SUM:4)
  END.
```

4.
```
  PROGRAM PRCDENCE (INPUT,OUTPUT);
  VAR
   CHTR1,CHTR2 : CHAR;
  BEGIN
   READLN (CHTR1,CHTR2);
   WRITE (' ',CHTR1,' ',CHTR2,'......');
   IF (CHTR1 = '*') OR (CHTR1 = '/') THEN
     IF (CHTR2 = '+') OR (CHTR2 = '-') THEN
       WRITELN (CHTR1,' HAS PRECEDENCE')
     ELSE
       WRITELN ('NEITHER HAS PRECEDENCE')
   ELSE IF (CHTR1 = '+') OR (CHTR1 = '-') THEN
     IF (CHTR2 = '*') OR (CHTR2 = '/') THEN
       WRITELN (CHTR2,' HAS PRECEDENCE')
     ELSE
        WRITELN ('NEITHER HAS PRECEDENCE')
  END.
```

5

Functions and Procedures

Functions and procedures are helpful in a program when your instructions become increasingly complex. A program becomes more readable—and it often can be written more concisely—by breaking it down into functions and procedures. Some functions and procedures are already built into Pascal and you need merely to refer to them by name, telling the computer what values or variables you wish to apply to your functions and procedures. Others you will need to define. This chapter reviews built-in functions and procedures and tells you how to define and call the ones that you create.

Built-in Functions

In previous chapters, you have seen some examples of built-in functions in Pascal, such as EOLN, EOF, SUCC. These functions carried out a particular task, by calling, or referring to, the built-in function of that name. If a set of parentheses containing a value or expression (its *argument*) follows the function name, the function then uses the argument in its computations. For example, SUCC ('Z') finds the value whose ordinal number succeeds the char value Z. Functions return only a single value, but they can be called over and over again with different arguments. For example:

```
SUCC ('Z');
SUCC ('9');
SUCC ('A');
```

The following is a list of the built-in functions of Standard Pascal, the value returned, and the types of arguments you can use with each one.

Built-in Function Name	Value Returned	Argument
ABS	The absolute value of the argument	real/integer
ARCTAN	The arctangent of the argument	real/integer (radians*)
CHR	A character whose ordinal number is the argument	integer
COS	The cosine of the argument	real/integer (radians)
EOF	Becomes true when the end of the file is reached; otherwise returns a value of false	file name†
EOLN	Becomes true when the end of a line of text is reached; otherwise returns a value of false	file name†
EXP	The value of e (2.718281828) to the power of the argument	real/integer
LN	The value of the logarithm of the argument in base e	real/integer (positive)

*π radians = 180 degrees

†If no file name follows the function name, the INPUT file is assumed to be the file referred to.

ODD	True if the argument has a value that is odd, and false if it is even	integer
ORD	The ordinal value of the argument	ordinal
PRED	The value whose ordinal number precedes the argument	ordinal
ROUND	The integer value nearest to a real argument	real
SIN	The sine of the argument	real/integer (radians)
SQR	The square of the argument	real/integer
SQRT	The square root of the argument	real/integer (positive or zero)
SUCC	The value whose ordinal number succeeds the argument	ordinal
TRUNC	The integer part of a real argument	real

ABS and SQR return a value that is either real or integer, depending upon the value of their argument. ROUND and TRUNC always return integer values. ARCTAN, COS, EXP, LN, SIN, and SQRT always return a real value whether the argument used is integer or real.

Built-in Procedures

The difference between a function and a procedure is that a function returns a single value; a procedure does not. For example, a function call may appear on the right side of an assignment statement, as in I := TRUNC (X);. The value returned from the built-in function TRUNC is assigned to the variable I. You cannot call a procedure from a statement that is an expression like you can a function. A procedure can be used either to compute several results or perform a task that does not involve computing any values.

READ, READLN, WRITE, and WRITELN are all actually built-in procedures. Other built-in procedures in Standard Pascal and the task that they perform are:

Built-in Procedure Name	Task Performed
NEW	Allocates memory space for a new node when using dynamic variables (see Chapter 8)
DISPOSE	Frees memory space no longer needed when using dynamic variables
GET	Transfers one record of a file to a buffer variable (see Appendix)
PUT	Adds the information in a buffer variable to its file
RESET	Opens a file so that it can be read (see Appendix)
REWRITE	Opens a file so that it can be written to

⌜PACK	Transfers data from an array to a packed array (see Chapter 6)
⌞UNPACK	Transfers data from a packed array to an unpacked array
PAGE	Causes a printer to skip to the top of the next page or a display device to be cleared with the cursor moved to the first column of the first row on the screen

Procedures used for complementary purposes are grouped in pairs. You do not have to understand the purposes of these built-in procedures at this point. You will encounter these procedures again in Chapters 6 and 8 and in the Appendix.

Defining Functions and Parameter Lists

You can create your own functions for programs by using the form:

```
FUNCTION FUNCTION-NAME (PARAMETER-LIST(S) :
        PARAMETER-TYPE) : FUNCTION-TYPE;
LOCAL DECLARATIONS (I.E. CONST,TYPE,VAR
        DECLARATIONS)
BEGIN
  STATEMENT-LIST
END;
```

FUNCTION tells the computer to expect a function of the name that follows. FUNCTION-NAME can be any valid identifier. The parameter list(s)—one or more variable names that correspond to the arguments used to call a function—are put in parentheses. If the function call has three values or variable names of type char as arguments, then your parameter list must have three corresponding—and compatible—variable names. Separate the lists of different types with semicolons. A parameter list enables you to use the function over and over again if you need to, substituting different values each time the function is called. If you do not use one or more arguments in parentheses as part of your function call, you do not need the parameter list(s) with parameter type and parentheses. FUNCTION-TYPE specifies the data type of the value returned by the function after the computations have been executed. This need not be the same data type as the parameter list.

You have the option of using *local* (within the function) declarations of any CONST, TYPE, or VAR identifiers that need to be defined only within the function. If you need the identifier outside of the function, the declaration should be outside of the function (*global* declaration). The rest of the function consists of the reserved words BEGIN and END surrounding a list of statements. One of the statements must assign a value to FUNCTION-NAME. This will be the value returned by the function.

Note that the reserved word END, which signals the end of the function, is followed by a semicolon. Use a period only at the very end of the entire program.

Function definitions are put near the beginning of the program, after your VAR declarations and before the reserved word BEGIN that marks the beginning of the main part of the program.

For example, the following function computes the volume of water needed to fill right cylindrical swimming pools. It is being called from the main program with a value of 14.2, corresponding to the radius of the pool and a value of 8.5, corresponding to the water level (height) of the pool. Always make sure the values or variable names in the arguments following your function call are in the same order as the corresponding parameters listed in the function declaration:

```
PROGRAM POOL (INPUT,OUTPUT);
 .
 .
 .
VAR
  VOL : REAL;
   .
   .
   .
FUNCTION VOLUME (RADIUS,HEIGHT : REAL) : REAL;
CONST
  PI = 3.14159; (*LOCAL DECLARATION*)
BEGIN
  VOLUME := PI * RADIUS * RADIUS * HEIGHT;
  WRITE ('RADIUS=',RADIUS:6:2,' HEIGHT=',HEIGHT:6:2)
END;
BEGIN (*MAIN PROGRAM*)
   .
   .
   .
  VOL := VOLUME (14.2,8.5);
  (*AFTER CALL TO FUNCTION, CONTROL IS PASSED*)
  (*BACK HERE TO STATEMENT FOLLOWING FUNCTION CALL*)
  WRITELN (' VOLUME=', VOL:8:2);
   .
   .
   .
END.
```

The output of this program would look like this:

```
RADIUS= 14.20 HEIGHT=   8.50 VOLUME= 5384.50
```

Defining Your Own Procedures

Remember that a procedure does not *return* any values—although values can be *passed* to the variables in the argument list of the procedure call. Unlike a function declaration, since a value is not returned, a procedure declaration has no equivalent to FUNCTION-TYPE. You are also not allowed to have a statement within the body of the procedure that assigns a value to PROCEDURE-NAME. Otherwise, a form similar to that for declaring functions is used to declare procedures:

```
PROCEDURE PROCEDURE-NAME (PARAMETER-LIST(S) : TYPE);
LOCAL DECLARATIONS
BEGIN
 STATEMENT-LIST
END;
```

Procedures, like functions, are put near the beginning of the program, after your VAR declarations and before the reserved word BEGIN that marks the beginning of the main part of the program.

Procedure calls take the form:

```
 PROCEDURE-NAME (ARGUMENT-LIST);
```

PROCEDURE-NAME must be a valid identifier. If you have no parameter list in your procedure declaration, omit the argument list and its parentheses in your procedure call. Remember that procedures, unlike functions, cannot be called from a statement that is an expression (such as VOL := VOLUME (14.2, 8.5);). The procedure call must be a separate statement.

Parameter lists in procedure declarations, as well as function declarations, can consist of either *variable parameters* (the reserved word VAR precedes the parameter list for each variable type), *value parameters* (not preceded by the reserved word VAR), or a combination of both. Separate each list and variable type with a semicolon.

Value parameters are local to the procedure or function. This means that a local variable receives each value in the argument of the procedure or function call, and, like variables in local declarations, these local variables are worked with in the procedure or function. Changes in values take place only within the procedure or function; they are not passed outside. This is the usual form you will want your function's parameters to take.

In a procedure, variable (VAR) parameters are useful as well. Variable parameters change the value of the actual variables manipulated by the procedure, even when control is passed outside the procedure. This is why only variables (and not constants or expressions) can be used as arguments passed to variable parameters. These variables must be of the same data type as their corresponding variable parameters in the parameter list in the procedure declaration. With value parameters, the corresponding part of the argument of the procedure call must be of *compatible* data type to the value parameter, but it does not necessarily have to be of the same data type. Depending upon the computer, variable parameters may take less memory space and processing time than value parameters do.

The next program demonstrates the difference between variable and value parameters. Procedures SUM1 and SUM2 are identical, except that SUM1 uses a value parameter. After the call to PROCEDURE SUM1 and the return in control to the main program, a new value for J will not have been passed outside the procedure. After the call to PROCEDURE SUM2, however, which uses a VAR parameter, and the return to the main program, a new value for J will have been passed outside the procedure:

```
PROGRAM DEMOPAR (OUTPUT);
CONST
 MAX = 10;
VAR
 I,J : INTEGER;
PROCEDURE SUM1 (PAR : INTEGER);
BEGIN
 PAR := 10;
 FOR I := 1 TO MAX DO
  PAR := PAR + I
END;
PROCEDURE SUM2 (VAR PAR : INTEGER);
BEGIN
 PAR := 10;
 FOR I := 1 TO MAX DO
  PAR := PAR + I
END;
```

```
BEGIN (*MAIN PROGRAM*)
  J := 100; (*INITIALIZE*)
  FOR I := 1 TO MAX DO
    J := J + I;
  (*INITIALIZE J TO 155*)
  WRITELN ('J INITIALIZED TO ',J:4);
  SUM1 (J);
  WRITELN ('J AFTER VALUE PARAMETER PASS ',J:4);
  (*J WILL NOT CHANGE FROM INITIALIZED VALUE*)
  SUM2 (J);
  WRITELN ('J AFTER VARIABLE PARAMETER PASS ',J:4)
  (*J WILL CHANGE HERE*)
END.
```

Nested Functions and Procedures:
For Complex Situations

Functions and procedures can be called from other functions and procedures, as well as from the main block of the program. A function or procedure can also call itself. This is called *recursion* (see Chapter 7). Functions and procedures can be nested within one another by placing the internal function or procedure after the local VAR declaration of the external function or procedure.

There are rules for calling one function or procedure from another. The called one must be declared before the function or procedure from which the call occurs. A function or procedure nested within another can only be called from the function or procedure that contains it.

Be very careful when you set up your declarations about which variable declarations are local and which are global. Also be careful about declaring value and variable parameters.

The next program demonstrates the use of a nested procedure. The program input is the amount of time in minutes it took you on each of a number of days last year to run three miles. PROCEDURE AVERAGE computes and prints your average running time per mile for the year. It is called from PROCEDURE DATAREAD, which reads the input file and computes the total running time that is to be used in computing an average per mile. PROCEDURE DATAREAD is called from the main program. You can see how several procedures can be listed before the main block of the program even begins. Note also that the main program block here is very short, consisting of only one procedure call.

```
PROGRAM RUNTIME (INPUT,OUTPUT);
PROCEDURE DATAREAD;
VAR
  MINUTES,SUM : REAL; (*LOCAL VARIABLES*)
  (*MINUTES IS MINUTES TO RUN THREE MILES*)
  DAYS : INTEGER;
  PROCEDURE AVERAGE (TOTAL : REAL;
    COUNT : INTEGER);
  VAR
    AV : REAL;
  BEGIN
    AV := TOTAL/(COUNT * 3);
    (*DIVIDE BY THREE TO GET AVERAGE TIME*)
    (*PER MILE. NOTE HOW PARENTHESES*)
    (*ESTABLISH PRECEDENCE OF OPERATORS*)
    WRITELN ('AVERAGE RUNNING TIME PER MILE = ',AV:5:2)
  END; (*PROCEDURE AVERAGE*)
BEGIN (*PROCEDURE DATAREAD*)
  SUM := 0; (*INITIALIZE*)
  DAYS := 0; (*COUNTER*)
  WHILE NOT EOF DO
    BEGIN
      READLN (MINUTES);
      DAYS := DAYS + 1;
      SUM := SUM + MINUTES
    END; (*WHILE-BEGIN*)
  AVERAGE (SUM,DAYS)
END; (*PROCEDURE DATAREAD*)
BEGIN (*MAIN PROGRAM*)
  DATAREAD
END.
```

Review Exercises

1. Using a function or procedure, write a program that searches for the highest average reading score in a list of schools' averages.

2. Using a procedure, write a program that converts letter grades to numeric grade points for a student and prints a total grade-point average and the number of credits a student has completed.

3. Using at least one function or procedure, write a program that keeps track of the total value of assets consisting of stocks and bank accounts.

Answers to Review Exercises

1.

```
PROGRAM MAXVALUE (INPUT,OUTPUT);
VAR
  READAVER : REAL;
PROCEDURE SEARCH (VAR MAXSCORE : REAL);
VAR
  AVERAGE : REAL;
BEGIN
  WHILE NOT EOF DO
    BEGIN
      READLN (AVERAGE);
      IF AVERAGE > MAXSCORE THEN
        MAXSCORE := AVERAGE
    END (*WHILE-BEGIN*)
END; (*PROCEDURE SEARCH*)
BEGIN (*MAIN PROGRAM*)
  READLN (READAVER);
  SEARCH (READAVER);
  WRITELN('HIGHEST AVERAGE = ',READAVER:5:1)
END.
```

2.

```
PROGRAM GPA (INPUT,OUTPUT);
VAR
  GRADE : CHAR;
  AVERAGE,GRAPOINT : REAL;
  CREDITS,CRED,PASSED : INTEGER;
  (*CREDITS IS CREDITS PER COURSE*)
  (*CRED IS CREDITS USED TO COMPUTE GPA*)
  (*PASSED IS TOTAL CREDITS PASSED*)
PROCEDURE CONVERT (VAR TOTALGPA : REAL; VAR
    TOTCRED,TOTPASS : INTEGER);
```

```
VAR
 POINTS : INTEGER;
BEGIN
 CASE GRADE OF
  'A' : POINTS := CREDITS * 4;
  'B' : POINTS := CREDITS * 3;
  'C' : POINTS := CREDITS * 2;
  'D' : POINTS := CREDITS * 1;
  'F','P','I','W' : POINTS := 0
 END; (*CASE*)
 TOTALGPA := TOTALGPA + POINTS;
 IF (GRADE <> 'P') AND (GRADE <> 'I') AND
   (GRADE <> 'W') THEN
  TOTCRED := TOTCRED + CREDITS;
 IF (GRADE <> 'F') AND (GRADE <> 'I') AND
   (GRADE <> 'W') THEN
  TOTPASS := TOTPASS + CREDITS
END; (*PROCEDURE CONVERT*)
BEGIN (*MAIN PROGRAM*)
 GRAPOINT := 0;
 CRED := 0;
 PASSED := 0;
 WHILE NOT EOF DO
  BEGIN
   READLN (GRADE,CREDITS);
   CONVERT (GRAPOINT,CRED,PASSED)
  END; (*WHILE-BEGIN*)
 AVERAGE := GRAPOINT/CRED;
 WRITELN ('GPA = ',AVERAGE:5:2);
 WRITELN ('TOTAL CREDITS PASSED = ',PASSED:5)
 END.
```

3.

```
PROGRAM NETWORTH (INPUT,OUTPUT);
VAR
 SAVINGS,ASSETS,STOCKTOT : REAL;
PROCEDURE STOCKS (VAR TOTALSTK : REAL);
VAR
 STKSHARE : INTEGER;
 STKWORTH : REAL;
BEGIN
 WHILE NOT EOF DO
  BEGIN
   READLN (STKSHARE,STKWORTH);
   (*READ NUMBER OF SHARES & MARKET*)
```

```
      (*PRICE OF EACH SHARE*)
      TOTALSTK := TOTALSTK + STKSHARE * STKWORTH
      (*MULTIPLY HAS OPERATOR PRECEDENCE HERE*)
    END (*WHILE-BEGIN*)
END; (*PROCEDURE STOCKS*)
FUNCTION BANKS (ACCOUNT : REAL) : REAL;
VAR
  CASH : REAL;
BEGIN
  CASH := 0;
  READLN (ACCOUNT);
  (*READ AMOUNT IN FIRST BANK ACCOUNT*)
  WHILE ACCOUNT > 0.0 DO
    BEGIN
      CASH := CASH + ACCOUNT;
      READLN (ACCOUNT)
      (*CONTINUE TO READ ACCOUNTS*)
    END; (*WHILE-BEGIN*)
  BANKS := CASH
END; (*FUNCTION BANKS*)
BEGIN (*MAIN PROGRAM*)
  ASSETS := BANKS (SAVINGS);
  (*NOTE FUNCTION CALL IN EXPRESSION*)
  STOCKTOT := 0;
  STOCKS (STOCKTOT);
  ASSETS := ASSETS + STOCKTOT;
  WRITELN ('TOTAL ASSETS = ',ASSETS:10:2)
END.
```

6

Data Structures:
Arrays, Records, and Sets

This chapter introduces three abstract data structures: *arrays, records*, and *sets*. When you deal with a large amount of data, these structures are useful in organizing and storing the data types discussed in the previous chapters. There are many other, more advanced data structures, but all are based upon these three.

Arrays: Processing Large Amounts of Data

The programs in previous chapters instruct the computer to read and perform various manipulations on a group of data values. This may be a simple process if there are three or ten values that you do not wish to store in memory, but it becomes cumbersome if you want to store in memory a list of 20 or 100 or 5,000 values.

In the programs that you have seen so far, as the computer reads each value of a variable, the previous value in that variable is lost. You cannot perform subsequent manipulations on those values. If you store these values in memory, you can perform manipulations on them later.

An array is a way to store values in memory, using the same variable name for each value. An array is useful, for example, if you want to find the average number of hours employees in a company work and then examine each employee's hours to see if they are above or below the average.

An array associates a series of memory locations with a variable name, rather than only one memory location that is used over and over again. An index is used to reference each value of the variable in the same array.

For example, for the array NUMBER:

Element	Indexed Variable	Value
1	NUMBER[1]	-3
2	NUMBER[2]	6
3	NUMBER[3]	15
4	NUMBER[4]	0
5	NUMBER[5]	-17
6	NUMBER[6]	41
7	NUMBER[7]	22
8	NUMBER[8]	10
9	NUMBER[9]	9
10	NUMBER[10]	-3

In this array, if the variable is named NUMBER, then NUMBER [8] means that you are referring to the eighth value in the array NUMBER. Note that this does not mean that the value of NUMBER in this location is equal to 8. The value may not even be numeric, although in the example the array is of integer type and the value of NUMBER [8] is 10. NUMBER [8] refers only to the location of the value. NUMBER [INDEX] refers to whatever location value is presently assigned to the variable INDEX.

You must declare arrays in your program. To declare arrays in the VAR section of your program, use the form:

VARIABLE-NAME : ARRAY [MIN-INDEX..MAX-INDEX] OF TYPE;

When you name your variable, you must follow the rules for naming identifiers that were noted in Chapter 1. MIN-

INDEX and MAX-INDEX are the minimum and maximum values of the index to the array locations. They can be any ordinal-type values; for example,

1..100, MINIMUM..MAXIMUM

(these must then be declared as constants), or 'A'..'Z'. You must also declare the data type of each value in the array locations. All of the values in an array must be of the same type, such as integer, real, or Boolean.

You can use any of the data types discussed so far. You can also use a TYPE declaration, along with a VAR declaration, to declare an array. For example, a string of text can be declared as an array of characters. An array of 100 character values can be declared in two ways:

```
VAR
  CHTR : ARRAY [1..100] OF CHAR;
```

or

```
TYPE
  ALPH = ARRAY [1..100] of CHAR;
VAR
  CHTR : ALPH;
```

In addition, you can make 1..100 constants in the CONST declaration:

```
CONST
  MINIMUM = 1;
  MAXIMUM = 100;
TYPE
  ALPH = ARRAY [MINIMUM..MAXIMUM] OF CHAR;
VAR
  CHTR : ALPH;
```

You can also declare these as a subrange, as in:

```
TYPE
  VALUES = 1..100;
  ALPH = ARRAY [VALUES] OF CHAR;
VAR
  CHTR : ALPH;
```

To work with individual element of an array, specify the location of the element using a particular index value.

As stated above, NUMBER [8] refers to the eighth value in
the array NUMBER. NUMBER [INDEX + 1] refers to the
seventh value in the array when INDEX is equal in value to
six. NUMBER [INDEX] + 1, on the other hand, adds one to
whatever value is located in array position 6. If the number in
NUMBER [6] equals 41 and the number in NUMBER [7]
equals 22, then, when INDEX equals 6, NUMBER [INDEX +
1] equals 22. NUMBER [INDEX] + 1 equals 42.

Often, you will want to work with *all* of the values in array
in sequence. Any of the loops in Chapter 3 can be used, but
many prefer the FOR loop for its conciseness. Suppose you
want to compute the average number of hours fifty employees
in a company worked in a particular week and then list the
array indices of all employees who worked more hours than
the average:

```
PROGRAM AVERAGE (INPUT,OUTPUT);
CONST
  MAXIMUM = 50;
TYPE
  HOURS = ARRAY [1..MAXIMUM] OF REAL;
VAR
  EMP : HOURS;
  INDEX : INTEGER; (*INDEX FOR ARRAY*)
  SUM,AV : REAL;
BEGIN
  SUM := 0;
  FOR INDEX := 1 TO MAXIMUM DO
    BEGIN
      READLN (EMP [INDEX]);
      SUM := SUM + EMP [INDEX]
    END; (*FOR-BEGIN*)
  AV := SUM/MAXIMUM; (*COMPUTES AVERAGE*)
  WRITELN ('AVERAGE HOURS WORKED =',AV:6:2);
  WRITELN ('ABOVE AVERAGE HOURS- WORKER NUMBER');
  FOR INDEX := 1 TO MAXIMUM DO
    IF EMP[INDEX] > AV THEN
      WRITELN (INDEX:4)
END.
```

In the program above, the first FOR loop goes through the
fifty locations in the array to read the numbers of hours each

employee worked that week. Since numbers of hours is of type real, the sum of hours for all employees is also of type real. The sum is accumulated through the loop and when the loop is exited, the average number of hours, also type real, is computed and printed. Since the number of hours each employee worked is now stored in the array, it is not necessary to reread this information to list those employees working more than the average number of hours. The second FOR loop searches the array to list index numbers of these workers.

If you want to work with only part of an array, use a loop that will terminate when it reaches a specified point or when it reaches the maximum size of the array.

Multidimensional Arrays: Extending the Array for Tables and Lists of More Than One Dimension

When storing characters in an array, a great deal of memory is wasted. This is the reason why PACKED ARRAYS are often used. Depending upon your computer's implementation of Pascal, a packed-array declaration may store data more compactly, although it may increase the amount of time the computer takes to execute your program. A packed-array declaration has the same form as an array declaration, but the word PACKED is added:

```
CHTR : PACKED ARRAY [1..100] OF CHAR;
```

You may want to use packed-array declarations when you have a two-dimensional array in which each array location stores another array. For example, a page of text with 24 lines and 80 columns can be declared as:

```
TYPE
  TEXTPAGE = PACKED ARRAY [1..24,1..80] OF CHAR;
VAR
  SINGLEPG : TEXTPAGE;
```

Note here that each row from 1 through 24 is a separate location in the array of row characters. Each location holds another array of 80 characters, which forms the column locations that make up lines of text on a page This can also be declared as:

```
SINGLEPG : ARRAY [1..24] OF ARRAY [1..80] OF CHAR;
```

or

```
SINGLEPG : ARRAY [1..24] OF PACKED ARRAY [1..80] OF CHAR;
```

Arrays can have even more than two dimensions. For example, to declare a three-dimensional array consisting of pages of rows and columns:

```
VAR
  BOOKPAGE : ARRAY [1..MAXIMUM] OF TEXTPAGE;
```

This could also be declared as:

```
BOOKPAGE : ARRAY [1..MAXIMUM,1..24,1..80] OF CHAR;
```

or

```
BOOKPAGE : ARRAY [1..MAXIMUM] OF ARRAY [1..24] OF ARRAY
  [1..80] OF CHAR;
```

Multidimensional arrays may consist of values other than characters. As with one-dimensional arrays, you can use any of the data types discussed so far.

When using multidimensional arrays, you will need a separate index to reference each array. For example, to read a list of states, a two-dimensional array, you will need an index for each state in the list and an index for each character in a state name. Let's use I and J for each these indices, respectively, in the following program, which reads a violent crime rate for each state and prints the names of those states below the national average:

```
PROGRAM STATES (INPUT,OUTPUT);
CONST
  MXSTAT = 50;
  MXNAM = 14;
  BLANK = ' '; (*SEE MODIFICATION OF PROGRAM BELOW*)
TYPE
  STATES = PACKED ARRAY [1..MXSTAT,1..MXNAM] OF CHAR;
  CRIMES = ARRAY [1..MXSTAT] OF REAL;
VAR
  STATNAME : STATES;
  CRIMRATE : CRIMES;
  I,J : INTEGER;
  AVERAGE,CRIMESUM : REAL;  (*AVERAGE RATE*)
BEGIN
  CRIMESUM := 0; (*INITIALIZE*)
  FOR I := 1 TO MXSTAT DO
   BEGIN
    FOR J := 1 to MXNAM DO
     READ (STATNAME [I,J]);
    READLN (CRIMRATE [I]);
    (*CRIMRATE IS ONE-DIMENSIONAL AND INPUTED*)
    (*ON SAME LINE AS STATNAME*)
    CRIMESUM := CRIMESUM + CRIMRATE [I]
   END; (*FOR-BEGIN*)
  AVERAGE := CRIMESUM / MXSTAT;
  FOR I := 1 TO MXSTAT DO
   IF CRIMRATE [I] < AVERAGE THEN
    FOR J := 1 to MXNAM DO
     WRITE (STATNAME [I,J])
END.
```

STATNAME [I,J] can also be referenced as STATNAME [I][J].

When entering the data in each array within the array—that
is, when entering each state name in STATNAME—each line
should consist of 14 characters, even if many of them are
spaces, as in "Maine   ', since that is how you declared
your array. Since this can make your data entry cumbersome,
you can use a marker value in entering data (such as '*') to sig-
nal the end of each state name. You can also pad the rest of
the array with blank characters as your computer reads the
data. For example:

```
FOR I := 1 to MXSTAT DO
  BEGIN
    J := 1;
    READ (STATNAME [I,J]);
    WHILE STATNAME [I,J] <> '*' DO
      BEGIN
        J := J + 1;
        READ (STATNAME [I,J])
      END; (*WHILE-BEGIN*)
    FOR K := J TO MXNAM DO
      STATNAME [I,K] := BLANK;
    READLN (CRIMRATE [I])
  END; (*FOR-BEGIN*)
```

I, J, and K are all used as index values here.

Records: Processing Information with Different Data Types

In the program segment PROGRAM STATES in the previous section, the two-dimensional array STATNAME was used to hold a list of states, and a one-dimensional array, CRIM-RATE, was used to hold a list of violent crime rates for each state. Since CRIMRATE data are of type integer and STAT-NAME data are of type char, these two items of information were in separate arrays, since an array can hold data of only one type. One advantage of records is that they can be used to store two related items of information, even though they are of different types.

To declare records in a VAR declaration, use the form:

```
VARIABLE-NAME : RECORD
  FIELD-NAME1 : TYPE;
  FIELD-NAME2 : TYPE;
    .
    .
    .
  FIELD-NAME-N : TYPE
END;
```

You can also declare a record using a TYPE declaration:

```
TYPE (*RESERVED WORD IN DECLARATION*)
  RECORD-NAME = RECORD
   FIELD-NAME1 : TYPE; (*SPECIFY TYPE HERE*)
   FIELD-NAME2 : TYPE;
   .
   .
   .
   FIELD-NAME-N : TYPE
  END;
VAR
  VARIABLE-NAME : RECORD-NAME;
```

When you name your variables, you must follow the rules for naming identifiers noted in Chapter 1. RECORD is a reserved word that tells the computer that a record is being declared. For each FIELD-NAME, you must fill in a name for each field in the record—that is, each record component. Each FIELD-NAME must be different and must be an identifier. TYPE is the data type you must specify for each corresponding field of the record. Any of the data types you have learned so far are valid types for record fields. For example:

```
TYPE
  STATES = RECORD
   NAME : PACKED ARRAY [1..MXNAM] OF CHAR;
   CRIMRATE : INTEGER
  END;
VAR
  STATNAME : STATES;
```

This tells the computer that STATNAME will be of type STATES, which is a record with two fields. The first field is a packed one-dimensional array of type char. The second field is an integer-type crime-rate figure. You can store the records for all fifty states by declaring an array of records. For example:

```
TYPE
  STATES = RECORD
   NAME : PACKED ARRAY [1..MXNAM] OF CHAR;
   CRIMRATE : INTEGER
  END;
VAR
  STATNAME : ARRAY [1..MXSTAT] OF STATES;
```

STATNAME [INDEX] then represents the record in the array referenced by INDEX. If INDEX has a value of three, STATNAME [INDEX] refers to the third record in the array. Remember that for all these declarations, MXNAM and MXSTAT must be declared as constants in your CONST section.

You usually will refer to and manipulate individual fields of a record in any one statement. (Sometimes an entire record can be manipulated at once with one statement, as in copying a record.) There are two ways to reference individual fields of a record. The first way:

```
VARIABLE-NAME.FIELD-NAME
```

Use a period between the variable name and the field name. For example, to reference the crime rate figure of the third state in the array:

```
STATNAME [3].CRIMRATE
```

STATNAME [3].NAME [2] references the second character of the name of the third state in the array.

The second way to reference individual fields is useful if you want to reference several fields of a record. You do not have to keep repeating the variable name. Instead, you use a WITH statement:

```
WITH VARIABLE-NAME DO
  BEGIN
    STATEMENT1;
    STATEMENT2;
    .
    .
    .
    STATEMENT-N
  END; (*WITH-BEGIN*)
```

In the statements contained in the WITH statement, only the field name is used. For example:

```
I := 1;
WITH STATNAME [I] DO
```

```
BEGIN
  FOR J := 1 TO MXNAM DO
    READ (NAME [J]);
  READLN (CRIMRATE)
END; (*WITH-BEGIN*)
```

If the WITH statement is within a FOR loop, you can reference individual fields of a record for an entire array of records. The next program segment illustrates this in PROCEDURE LEAP in the loop beginning FOR I := 1 TO 100 DO, which loops through an array of 100 records of names and years of birth to find those who were born in a leap year. It uses a mathematical trick for computing leap years—all years divisible by 400 or by 4, but not by 100. If a person's year of birth was in a leap year, a message is printed. Like packed arrays, packed records may save space.

```
PROGRAM CALCHECK (INPUT,OUTPUT);
TYPE
  BIRTHYR = PACKED RECORD
    NAME : PACKED ARRAY [1..15] CHAR;
    YEAR : 1582..1990
  END;
  DATETYPE = ARRAY [1..100] OF BIRTHYR;
VAR
  DATES : DATETYPE;
PROCEDURE LEAP;
VAR
  I,J : INTEGER; (*LOCAL VARIABLES*)
  LEAPYEAR : BOOLEAN;
BEGIN
  FOR I := 1 TO 100 DO
    WITH DATES [I] DO
      BEGIN
        FOR J := 1 TO 15 DO
          READ (NAME [J]);
        READLN (YEAR);
        IF YEAR MOD 400 = 0 THEN
          LEAPYEAR := TRUE
        ELSE IF (YEAR MOD 4=0) AND (YEAR MOD 100 <> 0) THEN
          LEAPYEAR := TRUE
        ELSE LEAPYEAR := FALSE;
        FOR J := 1 TO 15 DO
          WRITE (NAME [J]);
```

```
    IF LEAPYEAR = TRUE THEN
      WRITELN (' WAS BORN IN THE LEAPYEAR',YEAR:5)
    END (*WITH-BEGIN*)
 END; (*PROCEDURE LEAP*);
 PROCEDURE NEXTSUB (DA : DATETYPE);
 BEGIN

  .
  .
  .
 END; (*PROCEDURE NEXTSUB*)
 BEGIN
  LEAP; (*PROCEDURE CALL*)
  NEXTSUB (DATES);
  .
  .
  .
 END.
```

Other subroutines or parts of the main program should reuse
the data read into the above array. Otherwise, you would not
have to store the records in an array, because it would not
matter if previous record data were lost as new records were
read in.

Records Within Records: Storing Complex Data

In PROGRAM CALCHECK at the end of the previous section, a RECORD declaration contained fields for each person's
name and year of birth. Think about a hypothetical record
that contains fields for a person's name and day, month, and
year of birth, as well as a listing of the kind of employee position held and an employee number. Some of these fields are
more related than others and can be declared as records themselves. Day, month, and year of birth, for example, can form a
record within the larger record. Employee number and position can also form another record within the larger record. To
do this, the TYPE of the FIELD-NAME of the larger record
would be the RECORD-NAME of the internal record. For
example:

```
CONST
  MAX = 15;
TYPE
  DATEBRTH = RECORD
    DAY : 1..31;
    MONTH : 1..12;
    YEAR : 1880..1990
  END;
  EMPLOY = RECORD
    NUM : 1111..9999;
    KIND : (MANAGERIAL,SALES,CLERICAL,SKILLED,
        SEMISKILLED)
  END;
VAR
  PERSON : RECORD
    NAME : ARRAY [1..MAX] OF CHAR;
    BIRTH : DATEBRTH;
    EMP : EMPLOY
    (*DATEBRTH & EMPLOY ARE INTERNAL RECORD-NAMES*)
  END;
```

To refer to a field in a subrecord—NUM, example—you must also reference the field in the larger record that contains the subrecord. To reference NUM, use the form:

```
PERSON.EMP.NUM
```

You can use WITH statements with nested records to minimize repetition as you write your program. For example, to read and print an employee's number:

```
WITH PERSON.EMP DO
  BEGIN
    READLN (NUM);
    WRITELN ('EMPLOYEE NUMBER =',NUM:5)
  END;
```

When records are nested like this, you can also list the record and subrecord(s) in the WITH statement, separating each identifier by a comma. For example:

```
WITH PERSON, EMP DO
  BEGIN
    .
    .
    .
  END;
```

Suppose that you want to insert different information into the record. For example, with clerical, skilled, and semiskilled workers, you might want to know their hourly wages and the dates their employment began. With sales workers, you might want to know the value of successful sales so far this year and annual salaries. Or you might want to know only the annual salaries of managers.

You can include all of this information in a *variant* part of a record, using a CASE statement. Instead of using a variable label in the conventional CASE statement heading, a *tag* name is used, along with its type:

```
CASE TAG-NAME : TAG-TYPE OF
  TAG-VALUE1 :
   (FIELD-NAME1 : TYPE;
    .
    .
    .
   FIELD-NAME-N : TYPE);
  TAG-VALUE2 :
   (FIELD-NAME1 : TYPE;
    .
    .
    .
   FIELD-NAME-N : TYPE);
    .
    .
    .

  TAG-VALUE-N :
   (FIELD-NAME1 : TYPE;
    .
    .
    .
   FIELD-NAME-N : TYPE)
 END; (*USE ONLY ONE END TO MARK THE END OF BOTH*)
     (*THE VARIANT LIST AND THE ENTIRE RECORD*)
```

A variant part of a record is always positioned last in the record. Although record variants can be nested, there should be only one in a record. The record variant for employees can be declared as:

```
CONST
  MAX = 15;
TYPE
  KIND = (MANAGERIAL,SALES,CLERICAL,SKILLED,
      SEMISKILLED);
  DATEBRTH = RECORD
    DAY : 1..31;
    MONTH : 1..12;
    YEAR : 1880..1990
  END;
VAR
  PERSON : RECORD
    NAME : ARRAY [1..MAX] OF CHAR;
    NUM : INTEGER;
    BIRTH : DATEBRTH;
    CASE JOB : KIND OF
      MANAGERIAL :
        (SALARY1 : REAL);
      SALES :
        (SALEVAL : REAL;
         SALARY2 : REAL);
       CLERICAL,SKILLED,SEMISKILLED :
         (HRWAGE : REAL;
          STARTDAT : DATEBRTH)
  END;
```

Note that DATEBRTH can be used as a TYPE for more than one FIELD-NAME. But a FIELD-NAME should not be used more than once in the same record declaration.

If you use a record with a variant part, then you will need to take the variation into account when working with your records. When reading records in, for example, some fields will exist only on some records. You can use CASE statements in the body of your program to deal differently with variant records.

The next program segment demonstrates this, using the above record declaration for employees. It instructs the computer to read and print the record for an employee, taking into account that employees have variant records. It can be used to read and print a series of records if the records are declared as an array and the program segment is inserted into a loop that

traverses the array. In the program segment, note that a CASE
statement is used to convert JOBCODE into one of the
enumerated values of JOB, as well as to work with variants of
JOB once the conversion has taken place. Note also that
different field names (SALARY1 and SALARY2) are used to
label salary level for managerial and sales employees.

With this segment, you will need the additional declarations:

```
VAR
  I,THISYEAR,JOBCODE : INTEGER;
```

The program segment would be:

```
READLN (THISYEAR);
WITH PERSON DO
  BEGIN
    FOR I := 1 TO MAX DO
      BEGIN
        READ (NAME[I]);
        WRITE (NAME[I])
      END; (*FOR-BEGIN*)
    READLN (NUM);
    WRITELN (NUM:6);
    WITH BIRTH DO
      BEGIN
        READ (DAY,MONTH,YEAR);
        IF THISYEAR - YEAR >= 65 THEN
          WRITELN (' RETIREMENT CANDIDATE')
        ELSE
          WRITELN
      END; (*WITH-BEGIN*)
    READLN (JOBCODE);
    CASE JOBCODE OF
      1 : JOB := MANAGERIAL;
      2 : JOB := SALES;
      3 : JOB := CLERICAL;
      4 : JOB := SKILLED;
      5 : JOB := SEMISKILLED
    END; (*CASE*)
    CASE JOB OF
      CLERICAL,SKILLED,SEMISKILLED :
        BEGIN
          READ (HRWAGE);
          WRITE ('HOURLY WAGE IS',HRWAGE:6:2);
          WITH STARTDAT DO
```

```
      BEGIN
       READ (DAY,MONTH,YEAR);
       WRITELN ('STARTED',MONTH:3,DAY:3,YEAR:5)
      END (*WITH-BEGIN*)
    END; (*CLERICAL,ETC*)
   SALES :
    BEGIN
     READ (SALEVAL,SALARY2);
     WRITELN ('SOLD',SALEVAL:9:2,
       ' SAL',SALARY2:9:2)
    END; (*SALES*)
   MANAGERIAL :
    BEGIN
     READ (SALARY1);
     WRITELN ('SAL',SALARY1:9:2)
    END
  END (*CASE*)
 END; (*WITH BEGIN*)
```

Sets: Operations on Elements of the Same Collection

The relational operator IN tests if an item of data is a member of a specified set and yields a Boolean value—that is, true or false. This can be used to find out whether or not a data item is one of a group of values that are part of a collection.

Sets should be declared as follows, using both a TYPE and VAR declaration:

```
TYPE
 TYPE-NAME = SET-TYPE;
 SET-NAME = SET OF TYPE-NAME;
VAR
 VARIABLE-NAME : SET-NAME;
```

SET-TYPE must be an ordinal type and is usually a subrange or enumerated list of values. For example:

```
TYPE
 DAYS = (SUN,MON,TUES,WEDS,THUR,FRI,SAT);
 WEEK = SET OF DAYS; (*DAYS IS TYPE-NAME*)
VAR
 WEEKDAY,WEEKEND : WEEK; (*WEEK IS SET-NAME*)
```

```
BEGIN
  WEEKDAY : = [MON..FRI];
  WEEKEND : = [SAT,SUN];
  .
  .
  .
END;
```

A set value or group of values is enclosed in a bracket on the right-hand side of an assignment statement. These can be a list of values, a subrange, or the entire range of values in the set. A set can also be initialized as empty, using the empty brackets [ ].

In addition to the IN operator, several other operations are applicable to sets:

+   The set combines all of the elements belonging to *either* the set to the left or the set to the right of the operator

−   The set contains all the elements belonging to the set to the left and *not* the set to the right of the operator

*   The set with all elements belonging to *both* the set to the left and to the right of the operator

=   Boolean test of whether one set is *equal* to another set

<>   Boolean test of *inequality*

<=   Boolean test of whether the set to the left of the operator is *equal* to or a *subset* of the set to the right of the operator

>=   Boolean test of whether the set to the right of the operator is *equal* to or a *subset* of the set to the left of the operator

The IN Operator

For most simple programming purposes, the IN operator will be more useful than the operations above.

The next program illustrates the use of the IN operator with sets. The program instructs the computer to check if a day is a weekday or weekend and to pay double-time wages for the number of hours worked on a weekend. The total wages for the week are calculated. The program can also be used to calculate wages for a series of employees if an array of employees is declared and a loop is used to traverse the array:

```
PROGRAM PAYROLL (INPUT,OUTPUT);
TYPE
  DAYS = (SUN,MON,TUES,WEDS,THUR,FRI,SAT);
  WEEK = SET OF DAYS;
VAR
  WEEKDAY,WEEKEND : WEEK;
  DA : DAYS;
  WAGE,TOTWAGE,HOURS,HOURPAY : REAL;
BEGIN
  TOTWAGE := 0;
  (*TOTAL WEEKS WAGES INITILIZED*)
  WEEKDAY := [MON..FRI];
  WEEKEND := [SAT,SUN];
  READ (HOURPAY); (*HOURLY PAY*)
  FOR DA := SUN TO SAT DO
    BEGIN
      READLN (HOURS);
      CASE DA OF
        SUN : WRITE ('SUNDAY');
        MON : WRITE ('MONDAY');
        TUES: WRITE ('TUESDAY');
        WEDS: WRITE ('WEDNESDAY');
        THUR: WRITE ('THURSDAY');
        FRI : WRITE ('FRIDAY');
        SAT : WRITE ('SATURDAY')
      END; (*CASE*)
      IF DA IN WEEKDAY THEN
        WAGE := HOURS * HOURPAY (*DAILY WAGE*)
      ELSE
        WAGE := 2 * HOURS * HOURPAY;
        (*DOUBLE TIME DAILY WAGE*)
      WRITELN (WAGE:8:2);
      TOTWAGE := TOTWAGE + WAGE
    END; (*FOR-BEGIN*)
  WRITELN;
  WRITELN ('TOTAL WEEKLY WAGES ARE',TOTWAGE:8:2)
END.
```

To print each set member in this program, instructions for each value are contained within a CASE statement within a

FOR loop. The values in an entire set can be printed out by testing a range of values for membership in a set:

```
IF VARIABLE-NAME IN SET-NAME THEN
  STATEMENT;
```

You would then use a FOR loop to traverse the range of all possible values of VARIABLE-NAME.

For example, if you have a set consisting of all prime numbers between 1 and 100 called PRIMESET, then:

```
FOR NUMBER := 1 TO 100 DO
  IF NUMBER IN PRIMESET THEN
    WRITELN (NUMBER:5,' IS A PRIME NUMBER');
```

As with the other data structures discussed in this chapter, sets may save space if they are packed.

Review Exercises

1. A palindrome is a word or sentence whose characters are in the same order forward and backward (such as madam). To check for a palindrome, write a program to read a line of characters and print it both forward and backward, checking to see if the characters match.

2. Write a program to read a page of text and count the number of times the digits 1 through 9 appear.

3. Using procedures, write a program to combine two arrays of alphabetic characters in a third, larger array, keeping all of the characters in their original order (this is called *concatenation*).

4. Write a program to create a Dean's List for those students, out of the five hundred in the school, who have a grade-point index above 3.6 and who are at least sophomores (at least 32 credits completed).

5. A friend of yours asserts that a poet you both like uses an unusual number of certain consonants in her poems. Write

a program to read a line of characters from one of her poems and print the frequency of occurrence of each consonant.

6. Using a function, write a program that returns the smallest element of a set of integer values.

Answers to Review Exercises

1.

```
PROGRAM PRINTING (INPUT,OUTPUT);
CONST
 MAXIMUM = 80;
TYPE
 STRING = PACKED ARRAY [1..MAXIMUM] OF CHAR;
VAR
 SENTENCE : STRING;
 I,J,LENGTH : INTEGER;
 PALIND : BOOLEAN;
BEGIN
 PALIND := TRUE; (*INITIALIZATION*)
 I := 1;
 REPEAT
  READ (SENTENCE [I]);
  WRITE (SENTENCE [I]);
  I := I + 1
 UNTIL EOLN;
 WRITELN;
 LENGTH := I - 1;
 I := 1;
 FOR J := LENGTH DOWNTO 1 DO
  BEGIN
    WRITE (SENTENCE [J]);
    IF SENTENCE [J] <> SENTENCE [I] THEN
     PALIND := FALSE;
    I := I + 1
  END; (*FOR-BEGIN*)
 WRITELN;
 IF PALIND = TRUE THEN
  WRITELN ('WE HAVE A PALINDROME HERE')
  ELSE WRITELN ('THIS IS NOT A PALINDROME')
END.
```

2.

```
PROGRAM FREQ (INPUT,OUTPUT);
TYPE
```

```
      PG = PACKED ARRAY [1..24,1..80] OF CHAR;
      DIGITS = '1'..'9';
    VAR
      PAGE : PG;
      I,J : INTEGER;
      NUMBER,MINNUM,MAXNUM : DIGITS;
      COUNT : ARRAY [DIGITS] OF INTEGER;
    BEGIN
      MINNUM := '1';
      MAXNUM := '9';
      FOR NUMBER := MINNUM TO MAXNUM DO
       COUNT [NUMBER] := 0;
        (*INITIALIZE ARRAY*)
      WRITELN ('  DIGIT      FREQUENCY');
      FOR I := 1 TO 24 DO
        BEGIN
          FOR J := 1 TO 80 DO
           BEGIN
             READ (PAGE [I,J]);
             IF PAGE [I,J] IN ['1'..'9'] THEN
             (*NOTE THIS USE OF THE IN OPERATOR*)
               COUNT[PAGE[I,J]] := COUNT[PAGE[I,J]]+1;
               (*INCREMENT FREQUENCY FOR THAT DIGIT*)
           END; (*FOR J*)
          READLN
        END; (*FOR I*)
      FOR NUMBER := MINNUM TO MAXNUM DO
        WRITELN (NUMBER:6,COUNT[NUMBER]:5)
    END.
```

3.

```
    PROGRAM CONCAT (INPUT,OUTPUT);
    CONST
      MAX = 100; (*MAX ARRAY SIZE*)
    TYPE
      ARRREC = RECORD
        STRING : PACKED ARRAY [1..MAX] OF CHAR;
        STRSIZE : INTEGER
      END; (*RECORD*)
    VAR
      FIRSTSTR,SECSTR,THIRDSTR : ARRREC;
    PROCEDURE CAT (STRING1,STRING2 : ARRREC;
             VAR STRING3 : ARRREC);
    VAR
      I,LENGTH : INTEGER;
```

```
      BEGIN
        LENGTH := STRING1.STRSIZE;
        WITH STRING3 DO
          BEGIN
            FOR I := 1 TO STRING1.STRSIZE DO
              STRING [I] := STRING1.STRING [I];
            STRSIZE := LENGTH + STRING2.STRSIZE;
            FOR I := LENGTH + 1 TO STRSIZE DO
              STRING[I] := STRING2.STRING[I - LENGTH];
            FOR I := 1 TO STRSIZE DO
              WRITE (STRING[I])
          END (*WITH-BEGIN*)
      END; (*PROCEDURE*)
      PROCEDURE INP (VAR THESTRING : ARRREC);
      VAR
        J : INTEGER;
      BEGIN
        J := 1;
        READ (THESTRING.STRING [J]);
        WHILE THESTRING.STRING [J] <> '*' DO
          BEGIN
            J := J + 1;
            READ (THESTRING.STRING [J])
          END; (*WHILE-BEGIN*)
        THESTRING.STRSIZE := J - 1
      END;
      BEGIN (*MAIN PROGRAM*)
        INP (FIRSTSTR);
        INP (SECSTR);
        CAT (FIRSTR,SECSTR,THIRDSTR)
      END.
```

4.

```
PROGRAM DEANLIST (INPUT,OUTPUT);
CONST
  CUTOFF = 3.6; (*GPA NEDED FOR DEAN'S LIST*)
  SOPH = 32; (*CREDITS NEEDED*)
TYPE
  NAMETYPE = RECORD
    FIRST : PACKED ARRAY [1..10] OF CHAR;
    MIDDLE : CHAR;
    LAST : PACKED ARRAY [1..15] OF CHAR
  END;
  ST = RECORD
    NAME : NAMETYPE;
```

```
    GRADIND : REAL;
    CREDITS : INTEGER
  END;
VAR
  STUDENT : ST;
  J : INTEGER;
BEGIN
  WRITELN ('    DEANS LIST    ');
  WHILE NOT EOF DO
    WITH STUDENT,NAME DO
      BEGIN
        FOR J := 1 TO 10 DO
          READ (FIRST [J]);
        READ (MIDDLE);
        FOR J := 1 TO 15 DO
          READ (LAST [J]);
        READLN (GRADIND,CREDITS);
        IF (GRADIND>CUTOFF)AND(CREDITS>=SOPH) THEN
          BEGIN
            FOR J := 1 TO 10 DO
              IF FIRST [J] <> ' ' THEN
                WRITE (FIRST [J]);
              WRITE (' ',MIDDLE,'. ');
              FOR J := 1 TO 15 DO
                WRITE (LAST [J]);
              WRITELN (' GPA=',GRADIND:6:2,
                ' CREDITS=',CREDITS:5)
          END (*IF-BEGIN*)
      END (*WITH-STUDENT*)
END.
```

5.

```
      PROGRAM CONSONT (INPUT,OUTPUT);
      TYPE
        ALPHSET = SET OF 'A'..'Z';
      VAR
        ALPHABET, CONSNANT,VOW : ALPHSET;
        CHTR : CHAR;
        COUNT : ARRAY ['A'..'Z'] OF INTEGER;
      BEGIN
        ALPHABET := ['A'..'Z'];
        VOW := ['A','E','I','O','U'];
        CONSNANT := [ALPHABET]-[VOW];
        (*DIFFERENCE BETW. SETS TO DEFINE CONSONANTS*)
```

```
FOR CHTR := 'A' TO 'Z' DO
  COUNT [CHTR] := 0; (*INITIALIZE*)
WHILE NOT EOLN DO
  BEGIN
    READ (CHTR);
    WRITE (CHTR);
    COUNT [CHTR] := COUNT [CHTR] + 1;
  END; (*WHILE-BEGIN*)
WRITELN;
WRITELN ('CHARACTER COUNT');
FOR CHTR := 'A' TO 'Z' DO
  IF CHTR IN CONSNANT THEN
    WRITELN (CHTR,COUNT [CHTR]:6)
END.
```

6.

```
PROGRAM MINVALUE (INPUT,OUTPUT);
CONST
  LOW = 1;
  HIGH = 1000; (*RANGE OF POSSIBLE VALUES*)
TYPE
  VALUES = LOW..HIGH;
  SETTYPE = SET OF VALUES;
VAR
  ELEM : SETTYPE;
  NEXT,MIN: VALUES;
FUNCTION ELEMENT (SETELEM : SETTYPE) : VALUES;
VAR
  X : VALUES;
  FOUND : BOOLEAN;
BEGIN
  IF SETELEM = [ ] THEN
    WRITELN ('EMPTY SET')
  ELSE
    BEGIN
      FOUND := FALSE;
      X := LOW;
      WHILE (X <= HIGH) AND (NOT FOUND) DO
        IF X IN SETELEM THEN
          BEGIN
            ELEMENT := X;
            FOUND := TRUE
          END (*IF-BEGIN*)
        ELSE X := SUCC (X)
```

```
    END (*ELSE-BEGIN*)
END; (*FUNCTION*)
BEGIN (*MAIN PROGRAM*)
 ELEM := [ ];
 READLN (NEXT);
 WHILE NEXT <= 1000 DO
  BEGIN
   ELEM := ELEM + [NEXT];
   READLN (NEXT)
   END; (*WHILE-BEGIN*)
 MIN := ELEMENT (ELEM);
 WRITELN ('SMALLEST ELEMENT IS',MIN:5)
END.
```

7

Recursion

Remember from Chapter 5 that functions and procedures can call other functions and procedures, including themselves. Recursion is used when a function or procedure calls itself.

A recursive solution to a programming problem defines a function or procedure in terms of a simpler case of itself. Each time the function or procedure is called recursively, the problem being solved is simplified until a stopping point defined in the function or procedure is reached. At that point, earlier executions of the function or procedure are not yet complete and so the program travels back through all of the incomplete executions and completes their execution.

Factorial Computations and Backward Printing

Recursion can be illustrated by a function that obtains the factorial of a number. One of the review exercises in Chapter 3 was to write a factorial program and two suggested solutions were given, one using a FOR loop and the other using a WHILE loop. The repetition necessary to compute a factorial can also be programmed using recursive calls to a function. The recursive definition of a factorial function is (n is a positive integer):

1. The factorial of n equals one if n is zero.

2.   Otherwise, the factorial of n equals n multiplied by the factorial of n − 1.

To compute the factorial of a positive integer using recursion:

```
FUNCTION FACTORL (NUM: INTEGER) : INTEGER;
VAR
 NUM1,NUM2 : INTEGER;
BEGIN
 IF NUM = 0 THEN
   FACTORL := 1
 ELSE
   BEGIN
     NUM1 := NUM - 1;
     NUM2 := FACTORL (NUM1); (*RECURSIVE CALL*)
     FACTORL :=  NUM * NUM2
   END (*ELSE-BEGIN*)
END;
```

In the program above, the recursive solution to finding the factorial of a number is to look for the factorial of the number that is one less. This happens repetitively until the stopping point is reached where the number now equals zero. At that point, FACTORL is called with the argument NUM1 equal to zero and FACTORL is assigned a value of one. Each time the function is called, new space is allocated for the local variables and the value parameter. (This may mean the allocation of a lot of memory.) When the stopping point is reached, the computer must then return through all the function calls, each one retrieving the previous value of NUM, the parameter of the function. For example, if you want to find the factorial of five, the first function call assigns a value of five to NUM. The second function call, however, is made with the argument NUM1, which now has a value of NUM − 1, or four. On the next function call, NUM1 has a value of three, then two, then one, and finally zero, which stops the recursive calls.

FACTORL has now been assigned the value of one. Control now passes to the previous call of FUNCTION FACTORL, where the parameter passed to the function has a value of one, and back through all the preceding calls of FUNCTION FACTORL (NUM = 2, 3, 4, and 5) until FACTORL := NUM * NUM2 equals 120. The function returns to the point following that from which it was called. When writing recursive functions and procedures, always specify a simple case to stop the recursion. Otherwise, the recursive function or procedure will call itself continually and you will have an *infinite loop*.

Make sure that you understand the difference between the function call in the statement NUM2 := FACTORL (NUM1); and the assignment to the function name of a value in FACTORL := NUM * NUM2, which is not a function call.

Let's take a look at another example of recursion, a procedure that prints a line of characters backwards. One of the review exercises in Chapter 6 uses a FOR loop to do this. In the next program segment, when the recursive procedure is first called, the first character of the line of text is read. The procedure is called repeatedly, each successive character being read until the stopping condition, the end of the line, is reached. When going back through all the procedure calls in the order reverse to that in which they were originally called, the line of characters is printed backwards:

```
PROCEDURE REVERSE;
VAR
  CHTR : CHAR;
BEGIN
  READ (CHTR);
  IF NOT EOLN THEN
    REVERSE;
  WRITELN (CHTR)
END; (*PROCEDURE REVERSE*)
```

The following diagrams illustrate what happens as successive recursive calls to PROCEDURE REVERSE proceed. Let's use as sample data input the string. THIS IS A SAMPLE LINE OF CHARACTERS. After the first call to PROCEDURE

REVERSE, the character T has been read. Although the procedure contains an instruction to print the character, nothing is yet printed, because since it is NOT EOLN, the first execution of PROCEDURE REVERSE is temporarily interrupted and PROCEDURE REVERSE is called again and the character H is read. Now two sets of the local variable CHTR are stacked one on top of the other.

Copies of Local Variable CHTR

H
T

As each character is read by another call to PROCEDURE REVERSE, the copies of the local variable CHTR will eventually look like this:

Copies of Local Variable CHTR

.
S
R
E
T
C
A
R
A
H
C

F
O

E
N
I
L

E
L
P
M
A
S

A

S
I

S
I
H
T

After all of the characters on the line have been read, EOLN is now true and recursive calls to PROCEDURE REVERSE stop. At this point, control passes to the next statement in the procedure, WRITELN (CHTR). The most recent copy of CHTR, '.', is printed; that is, the copy of CHTR at the top of the stack. Each return from PROCEDURE REVERSE is to a point in the previous procedure call. The most recent copy of the local variable is retrieved and subsequently printed. This continues through each copy of the local variable until all copies have been retrieved and printed. If there were any other local declarations or any value parameters in the procedure, they would be copied and retrieved along with the local variable CHTR.

Binary Search: A Method for Searching Arrays

A function commonly used to illustrate recursion is one for
conducting a binary search. Binary search looks for an element in an ordered array. It does this by finding a middle
index value in the array, averaging the lowest and highest
value, using integer division (DIV). IF the element being
searched for is lower in value than the middle value, only the
lower half of the array is searched. If the element being
searched for, however, is higher in value than the middle
value, then the upper half of the array is searched. The search
conducted on half of the array is also a binary search. A middle index value is located and half of the arrayhalf is searched,
again using a binary search. This procedure lends itself easily
to a recursive programming solution. The stopping condition
is that the element is found in the array, in which case its index
position in the array is returned as the value of the function, or
the element is not in the array, in which case LO > HI and a
value of zero is returned as the value of the function. The
recursive function BINARY is called from the nonrecursive
function SEARCH. FUNCTION BINARY's parameters LO
and HI are reset at each recursive call, so that the upper and
lower boundaries of the array portion searched are changed
each time. You do not have to search the entire array every
time you recursively go through the array. You need only
search half of the portion of the array that you searched last
time FUNCTION BINARY was called.

```
FUNCTION SEARCH (ARR : VALARRAY;I,INT : INTEGER) : INTEGER;
FUNCTION BINARY (LO,HI : INTEGER) : INTEGER;
VAR
  MIDDLE : INTEGER;
BEGIN
  IF LO > HI THEN
    BINARY := 0
    (*ONE OF THE STOPPING CONDITIONS*)
    (*ELEMENT NOT FOUND*)
  ELSE
```

```
  BEGIN
    MIDDLE := (LO + HI) DIV 2;
    IF INT = ARR [MIDDLE] THEN
      BINARY := MIDDLE
      (*ELEMENT FOUND - STOPPING CONDITION*)
    ELSE IF INT < ARR [MIDDLE] THEN
      BINARY := BINARY (LO,MIDDLE - 1)
    ELSE
      BINARY := BINARY (MIDDLE + 1,HI)
  END (*ELSE-BEGIN*)
END; (*FUNCTION BINARY*)
BEGIN (*FUNCTION SEARCH*)
  SEARCH := BINARY (1,I)
END; (*FUNCTION SEARCH*)
```

Quicksort: A Method for Sorting Arrays

Quicksort is a binary sorting technique that uses a model similar to the binary search to sort an array instead of to search it. To sort an array is to order the values stored in the array.

Quicksort picks a pivotal value around which the other elements of the array will be sorted. Quicksort is then applied recursively to all values less than the pivotal value and to all values greater than the pivotal value until the array is sorted. The next program demonstrates quicksort, using a recursive procedure called QUICK. PROCEDURE QUICK calls two functions—FUNCTION FIND and FUNCTION DIVIDE. FUNCTION FIND locates the index to the pivotal value that each time recursively divides the array. FUNCTION DIVIDE swaps array elements so that those values less than the pivotal value are on the left side and those values greater than or equal to the pivotal value are on the right side. The function returns the beginning index to those values to the right of the pivotal value.

```
PROGRAM SORTARRS (INPUT,OUTPUT);
CONST
  ARRSIZE = 100;
TYPE
  SORTARR = ARRAY [1..ARRSIZE] OF INTEGER;
```

```pascal
VAR
 I : INTEGER;
 ARR : SORTARR;
FUNCTION FIND (I,J : INTEGER) : INTEGER;
(*IF IDENTICAL VALUES FOR ARR[I],...,ARR[J] THEN*)
(*FUNCTION RETURNS A ZERO. OTHERWISE FUNCTION*)
(*RETURNS THE ARRAY INDEX OF THE LARGER OF THE*)
(*LEFTMOST TWO VALUES*)
LABEL
 999;
VAR
 VALUE : INTEGER;
 K : INTEGER; (*INDEX TO SCAN FOR LOOP*)
BEGIN
 VALUE := ARR [I];
 FOR K := I + 1 TO J DO
  IF ARR [ K ] > VALUE THEN
   BEGIN
    (*LARGER PIV SELECTED*)
    FIND := K;
    GOTO 999
   END (*IF-BEGIN*)
  ELSE IF ARR [K] < VALUE THEN
   BEGIN
    FIND := I;
    GOTO 999
   END; (*ELSE-BEGIN*)
  FIND := 0;
  999 :
END; (*FUNCTION FIND*)
FUNCTION DIVIDE (I,J,PIV : INTEGER) : INTEGER;
(*DIVIDES ARR[I],...ARR[J] SO THAT ARRAY INDICES*)
(*OF ELEMENTS < PIV ARE AT THE LEFT AND ARRAY*)
(*INDICES OF ELEMENTS >= PIV ARE ON THE RIGHT*)
(*FUNCTION RETURNS THE BEGINNING OF RIGHT-SIDE GROUP*)
VAR
 TEMP,L,R : INTEGER; (*L & R = LEFT AND RIGHT*)
BEGIN
 L := I;
 R := J;
 REPEAT
  TEMP := ARR [L];
  ARR [L] := ARR [R];
  ARR [R] := TEMP;
```

```
  (*THIS SWAPS THE VALUES*)
  WHILE ARR [L] < PIV DO
    L := L + 1;
  WHILE ARR [R] >= PIV DO
    R := R - 1
 UNTIL L > R;
 DIVIDE := L
END; (*FUNCTION DIVIDE*)
PROCEDURE QUICK (I,J : INTEGER);
VAR
 PIV,PIVINDEX,K : INTEGER;
 (*K IS BEGINNING INDEX OF ELEMENTS >= PIV*)
BEGIN
 PIVINDEX := FIND (I,J);
 IF PIVINDEX <> 0 THEN
   BEGIN (*ELSE DO NOTHING*)
     PIV := ARR [PIVINDEX];
     K := DIVIDE (I,J,PIV);
     QUICK (I,K-1); (*RECURSION*)
     QUICK (K,J)
   END (*IF-BEGIN*)
END; (*PROCEDURE QUICK*)
BEGIN (*MAIN PROGRAM*)
 FOR I := 1 TO ARRSIZE DO
   READLN (ARR [I]);
 QUICK (1, ARRSIZE);
 (*CALLS PROCEDURE QUICK*)
 FOR I := 1 TO ARRSIZE DO
   WRITELN (ARR [I]:6)
END.
```

Review Exercises

1. Write a recursive function that returns the value of a number to the nth power.

2. Write a recursive function that returns the sum of all even integers from zero to NUM if NUM is even and the sum of all odd integers from 1 to NUM if NUM is odd.

3. Write a recursive procedure to print in order all of the integers from a specified minimum value to a specified maximum value.

4. The Fibonacci sequence is a sequence of integers in which each integer is the sum of the two preceding ones. It begins as:

```
0,1,1,2,3,5,8,13,21,34,55 . . .
```

Write a recursive function to compute the nth Fibonacci number.

Answers to Review Exercises

1.
```
FUNCTION POWERS (NUM,N : INTEGER) : INTEGER;
BEGIN
  IF N = 0 THEN
    POWERS := 1
  ELSE
    POWERS := POWERS (NUM,N-1) * NUM
END;
```

2.
```
FUNCTION SUMNUMS (NUM : INTEGER) : INTEGER;
BEGIN
  IF (NUM = 0) OR (NUM = 1) THEN
    SUMNUMS := NUM
  ELSE
    SUMNUMS := NUM + SUMNUMS (NUM-2)
END;
```

3.
```
PROCEDURE PRINTNUM (MIN,MAX : INTEGER);
BEGIN
  IF MAX <> MIN THEN
    PRINTNUM (MIN,MAX - 1);
  WRITELN (MAX :4)
END;
```

4.
```
FUNCTION FIBO (N : INTEGER) : INTEGER;
BEGIN
  IF N <= 1 THEN
    FIBO := N
  ELSE
    FIBO :=FIBO (N-1) + FIBO (N-2)
END;
```

8

Pointers

In previous chapters, examples of arrays of records or of other forms of data have remained stable in size. In a real-life situation, however, the number of elements may change constantly. In a business, for example, turnover affects the number of employees and their specific characteristics at any given time. If your employee list is in alphabetical order and an employee quits, all of the records in the array that followed alphabetically would have to be moved back one index value to fill the gap left by the departing employee. Similarly, if a new employee were later hired, a gap in the array would have to be created in order to list the new employee alphabetically in the array. All of the records following alphabetically would again have to be moved, this time forward one index value. In a constantly changing list, this would entail a great deal of moving back and forth.

Another potential disadvantage of arrays is that the number of array positions needed must be declared in advance. The amount of storage allocated then remains fixed and cannot be used for anything else, even if it is not being entirely used in your program. Also, you then have to be careful that the elements in your data do not exceed the number that you have declared for your array.

Pascal has another, more flexible, way to maintain constantly changing lists: *pointers* to dynamic variables. A pointer points to a particular storage location, or address, in memory.

In Figure 8.1, P, Q, and R are pointers to locations in memory. P points to one location. Q and R both point to another location.

The number of addresses used to store values of the dynamic variable can expand and contract constantly, depending upon how many memory locations you need. This expansion and contraction can occur during the execution of the program and does not need to be defined in advance. Instead, if you must add a record to the list, you can create a new node and put it in its proper alphabetical order between two existing nodes. If a record has to be removed from the list, an existing node, representing the record, can be removed and all other records can remain.

Each node, created as needed, may contain a record that includes a pointer to the storage location of the next node, as shown in Figure 8.2. All of the nodes in the list are linked together.

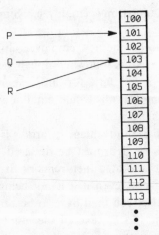

Figure 8.1.   Pointers and a section of memory locations.

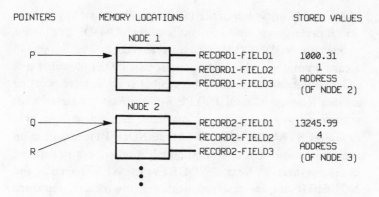

Figure 8.2. Linking dynamic records

Nodes can contain other information as well—for example, the storage location of a previous node or several subsequent nodes—but here you will be introduced to the simplest case of a node containing a record that includes a pointer to the next node.

Declaring Dynamic Variables: Creating and Using Dynamic Data Structures

Pointers and the records they point to in memory can be declared using the syntactic form:

```
TYPE
  NODEPTR = ^NODETYPE;
  NODETYPE = RECORD
    FIELD-NAME1 : TYPE;
    FIELD-NAME2 : TYPE;
    .
    .
    .
    NEXTNODE   : NODEPTR
  END;
VAR
  VARIABLE-NAME : NODEPTR;
```

A variable of type NODEPTR is named. According to your
TYPE declarations, this means it is of type ^NODETYPE, or a
pointer to NODETYPE, which is a record. The symbol ^
means a pointer to the object represented by the identifier that
follows. (On some systems, the symbol is an upward-pointing
arrow.) The record NODETYPE will consist of whatever fields
are relevant to your particular problem, including a field, here
called NEXTNODE, which is of type NODEPTR, a pointer to
the next record in your list. Although they are not underlined
in the syntactic form, NODETYPE, NEXTNODE, and
NODEPTR are *not* reserved words or predefined identifiers.
You can use any valid identifiers in place of them. However,
the syntactic form provides a declaration that you can use by
filling in only your own variable name and the name and type
of each field of the record other than NEXTNODE.

When VARIABLE-NAME is referred to in the body of your
program, it is a pointer and, as such, should not be assigned a
value other than that of another pointer. The only other
operations allowed on the pointers themselves are comparisons
for equality and inequality—for example, if you want to see if
two pointers point to the same memory location. To assign a
value to the variable to which VARIABLE-NAME points, you
must use the form:

`VARIABLE-NAME^`

The symbol ^ indicates the variable to which VARIABLE-
NAME points. Without this symbol, it refers to the pointer.
To refer to the first field of the record pointed to by
VARIABLE-NAME, for example, use the form

`VARIABLE-NAME ^. FIELD-NAME1;`

The following variable declarations illustrate the use of the
dynamic-variable-declaration form. This is a dynamic-variable
version of a list of names:

```
TYPE
  NODEPTR = ^NODETYPE;
  NODETYPE = RECORD
    FIRST : PACKED ARRAY [1..10] OF CHAR;
    MIDDLE : CHAR;
    LAST : PACKED ARRAY [1..15] OF CHAR;
    NEXTNODE : NODEPTR
  END;
VAR
  NAME : NODEPTR;
```

Creating and Disposing of Nodes

Since the number of records used during the execution of a program is flexible when dynamic variables and pointers are used, you need a means for allocating memory space to the dynamic variable. This is done by using one of the built-in procedures in Chapter 5. NEW (<u>ARGUMENT</u>) calls the standard procedure NEW. This allocates storage space for the variable pointed to by the argument and assigns the address in memory of that variable value or data structure to the argument. For example, NEW (NAME); would allocate space for a record pointed to by NAME of type NODETYPE and assign the address to NAME. Values could then be assigned to each of the fields of the record pointed to by NAME as follows:

```
NAME^.FIRST := 'SUSAN     ';
NAME^.MIDDLE := 'H';
NAME^.LAST := 'GRAY          ';
```

Note that the record fields to which the pointer points, NAME^, are assigned values. NAME, the pointer, is not.

The address in NAME can be assigned to another declared pointer. IF NEXTNAME were also declared in your variable declarations as being of type NODEPTR, the assignment statement NEXTNAME := NAME; would be valid. Both pointers must point to a variable or data structure of the same type.

NAME^ can refer to different records at different times. In
the illustration above, I have assigned my name to the fields in
the record pointed to by NAME. However, as the value of
NAME changes in the program, the values in NAME^, the
record pointed to by NAME, change as well.

For example, in the next program segment, as new nodes are
created, they are assigned different values. All the nodes are
created by the same procedure call, NEW (NAME);, but each
NAME represents a different memory location and, conse-
quently, each time points to a different NAME record:

```
NEXTNAME := NAME;
NEW (NAME);
NAME^.FIRST := 'FREDDY      ';
NAME^.MIDDLE := 'D';
NAME^.LAST := 'HOFFMANN-GRAY ';
```

The memory location originally pointed to by NAME is now
stored in NEXTNAME, so NEXTNAME now points to the
record storing SUSAN H. GRAY. At this point, if you assign a
different value to any of the fields of NEXTNAME^, you are
also changing the value of those same fields in NAME^, and
vice versa. This situation changes in the next line, once a new
node is created, in which the first record field stores the array
'FREDDY   '. The first record field of NEXTNAME^ is
still SUSAN. If the memory location originally pointed to by
NAME were not reassigned to NEXTNAME, you would have
no means of referring to it once you created a new node.

The next program segment reads as input the character
values that are then assigned to the field, FIRST, of the record
pointed to by NAME:

```
For I := 1 TO 10 DO
  READ (INP [I]);
NEW (NAME);
NAME^.FIRST := INP;
```

Another built-in procedure presented in Chapter 5,
DISPOSE (<u>ARGUMENT</u>);, frees the storage previously

pointed to by ARGUMENT and makes it available for reuse. You cannot, however, then use or make an assignment to the variable pointed to by that pointer until another NEW (<u>ARGUMENT</u>) is executed. For example,

```
DISPOSE (NAME);
NAME^.FIRST := NEXTNAME^.FIRST;
```

is not valid. You have disposed of the pointer currently in NAME and therefore the computer has no record pointed to by NAME until you assign another value to name, using NEW (NAME);. However,

```
DISPOSE (NAME);
NAME := NEXTNAME;
```

is valid because you are assigning to NAME the pointer value already in NEXTNAME.

The next program uses pointers to print the letters of the alphabet. Although there are simpler ways to do this, the program illustrates many of the principles discussed above to help you understand how to apply pointers and dynamic variables to solve a straightforward problem.

Nodes are created and each one holds a record consisting of a character value and a pointer to the next node. Each letter of the alphabet is entered into a node using the FOR loop, which also arranges the letters in nodes connected sequentially. Record field values for the field NOD^.CHTR1, which contain the alphabetic characters, are then printed out in the WHILE loop. The unnecessary nodes are disposed of along the way.

```
PROGRAM ALPHBET (OUTPUT);
TYPE
  NODEPTR = ^NODETYPE;
  NODETYPE = RECORD
    CHTR1 : CHAR;
    NEXT : NODEPTR
  END;
VAR
  NOD,P,Q : NODEPTR;
  CHTR2 : CHAR;
```

```
BEGIN
 NEW (NOD);
 Q := NOD;
 FOR CHTR2 := 'A' TO 'Z' DO
  BEGIN
   Q^.CHTR1 := CHTR2;
   P := Q;
   NEW (Q);
   P^.NEXT := Q
  END; (*FOR-BEGIN*)
 DISPOSE (Q);
 P^.NEXT := NIL;
 WHILE NOD <> NIL DO
  BEGIN
   WITH NOD^ DO
    BEGIN
     WRITE (CHTR1);
     Q := NEXT
    END; (*WITH-BEGIN*)
   DISPOSE (NOD);
   NOD := Q
  END (*WHILE-BEGIN*)
END.
```

The program above uses the reserved word NIL in the lines P^.NEXT := NIL; and WHILE NOD <> NIL DO. The pointer value NIL indicates that there are no more nodes. This program uses a data structure called a *linked list* to create nodes which are connected to facilitate searching all of the records created. Linked lists usually contain the pointer value NIL as the last pointer value at the end of the list.

Linked Lists:
Creating a List of Connected Nodes

A linked list orders a collection of values or records. Each value or record is located in a node, and each node contains a pointer to the address in memory of the next node in the list. This way, if you can access the *head* pointer, an external pointer that is not part of a node record but contains only the location in memory of the first node on the list, you can traverse the whole list. The NEXTNODE field of the last node on the list has the value NIL. This indicates the end of the list; it is not an actual address. When a list is completely empty, the head pointer's value is NIL.

Figure 8.3 shows a linked list of three nodes, the beginning of the list pointed to by a head pointer.

Each node is linearly linked by means of the pointer to the next node. The final node contains the pointer value NIL, which signals the end of the list.

Since all of the nodes are linked in this way, when you insert a new node, you must modify the linkages so that the list remains connected. If the list is ordered, you may wish to insert a node into the middle of the list to maintain the order rather than adding it at the end. Similarly, in constructing the list, if you wish to construct an ordered list, nodes will be created and inserted into the middle of a sequence of other nodes.

To insert a node into a linked list, use the following set of statements. Two pointers, P and Q, are used. P points to the

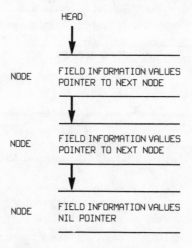

Figure 8.3.   Linked list of nodes

node that precedes the node that you want to insert. Q points
to the new node:

```
NEW (Q);
Q^.FIELD1 := INP1;
Q^.FIELD2 := INP2;
Q^.NEXTNODE := P^.NEXTNODE;
P^.NEXTNODE := Q;
```

A new node is created using the built-in procedure NEW.
INP1 and INP2 are two pieces of input assigned to the first two
fields of the record of the new node pointed to by Q. The field
that points to the next node on the linked list is then made to
point to the node that originally followed P^. It now follows
Q^ because Q^ was inserted after P^. The field of P^ that
points to the node following P^ is then changed to point to Q^,
as shown in Figure 8.4.

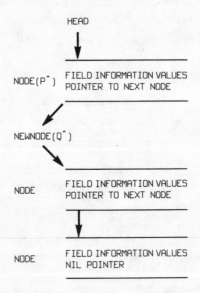

Figure 8.4.   Inserting a new node into a linked list

If you insert the node to the front of the list, you must change the value of the external pointer so that it points to the new node. For example:

```
NEW (Q);
Q^.FIELD1 := INP1;
Q^.FIELD2 := INP2;
Q^.NEXTNODE := HEAD;
HEAD := Q;
```

Figure 8.5 illustrates what happens during this sequence of statements.

Just as you must maintain the order of the linked list when you insert a new node, you must maintain the order of the list when you delete a node. The next program segment illustrates a method for deleting a node. First the list is searched for the record to be deleted (you are looking for the record whose first

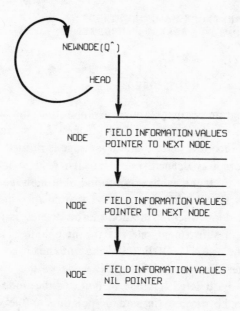

Figure 8.5.   Inserting a new node to the front of the list

field equals X). If that record is in the list, it is deleted, relink-
ing the list.

```
Q := HEAD;
FOUND := FALSE;
WHILE (Q <> NIL) AND NOT FOUND DO
  BEGIN
    IF Q^.FIELD1 = X THEN
      FOUND := TRUE
    ELSE
      BEGIN
        P := Q;
        Q := Q^.NEXTNODE
        (*ADVANCES THROUGH LIST TO CONTINUE SEARCH*)
      END (*ELSE-BEGIN*)
  END; (*WHILE-BEGIN*)
IF FOUND THEN
  BEGIN
    IF Q = HEAD THEN
      HEAD := Q^.NEXTNODE
    ELSE
      P^.NEXTNODE := Q^.NEXTNODE;
    WRITELN (Q^.FIELD1,' DELETED');
    DISPOSE (Q)
  END (*IF-BEGIN*)
ELSE
  WRITELN (X,' NOT FOUND');
```

The program segment above assumes that the identifying
field of the record is the first field. If the value searched for is
found, the record is deleted and a message is printed indicating
which record was deleted, using the first field to identify the
whole record. If the value is not found, that message is printed
as well. A slightly different method is used to relink the list,
depending upon whether the node to be deleted is the first in
the list or a subsequent one. If the first node in the list is
deleted, the NEXTNODE following the head is made the
head. Otherwise, the NEXTNODE value of the node before
the one to be deleted is made to point to the node following
the one to be deleted (instead of pointing to the one being
deleted, as it does before deletion).

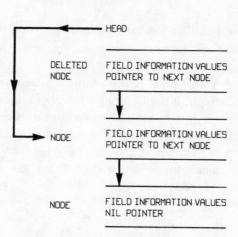

Figure 8.6.   Deleting the first node of a list

Figures 8.6 and 8.7 illustrate both deletion processes. In Figure 8.6, the first node is deleted and the head now points to what was previously the second record on the list.

In Figure 8.7, a middle node is deleted, with the corresponding linkage changes made that were described above.

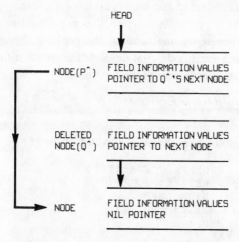

Figure 8.7.   Deleting a middle node of a list

Put these insertion and deletion segments into procedures, because they will be used a lot when you use dynamic variables.

The linearly linked lists in this chapter have some shortcomings. For example, it is difficult to get access to nodes that precede an arbitrary place in the list. You must traverse the list in order from the beginning. More sophisticated data structures based upon the same principles can be used, such as circular linked lists, doubly linked lists, and trees, but they are beyond the scope of this book.

Review Exercises

1.   Using pointers, write a program to reverse characters in a line of text.

2.   Assume a linked list in which the last record in the list contains a pointer to the first record in the list, instead of a pointer to NIL. Write a procedure to print the two information fields of each record, one of which is an array of char values, and the other of which is an integer value.

3.   Write a recursive function that copies a linked list and returns a pointer to the head of the copy of the original list. Assume that each node contains one information field of type real, as well as a pointer to the next node.

Answers to Review Exercises

1.

```
PROGRAM REVERSE (INPUT,OUTPUT);
TYPE
  NODEPTR = ^NODETYPE;
  NODETYPE = RECORD
    CHTR : CHAR;
    NEXTCH : NODEPTR
  END;
VAR
  NOD,BEG : NODEPTR;
```

```
BEGIN
 BEG := NIL;
 WHILE NOT EOLN DO
  BEGIN
   NEW (NOD);
   READ (NOD^.CHTR);
   NOD^.NEXTCH := BEG;
   BEG := NOD
  END; (*WHILE-BEGIN*)
 NOD := BEG;
 WHILE NOD <> NIL DO
  BEGIN
   WRITE (NOD^.CHTR);
   NOD := NOD^.NEXTCH
  END;
 WRITELN
END.
```

2.

The program declarations:

```
CONST
 MAX = 10;
TYPE
 NODEPTR = ^NODETYPE;
 NODETYPE = RECORD
  INFO1 : ARRAY [1..MAX] OF CHAR;
  INFO2 : INTEGER;
  NEXTNODE : NODEPTR
 END;
```

The procedure:

```
PROCEDURE PRINTED (R : NODEPTR);
VAR
 I : INTEGER;
 Q : NODEPTR;
BEGIN
 IF R <> NIL THEN
  BEGIN
  (*LIST IS NOT EMPTY*)
   Q := R;
   REPEAT
    Q := Q^.NEXTNODE;
    FOR I := 1 TO MAX DO
```

```
        WRITE (Q^.INFO1[I]);
         WRITELN (' ',Q^.INFO2)
       UNTIL Q = R
     END (*IF-BEGIN*)
  END;
```

3.

The program declarations:

```
TYPE
  NODEPTR = ^NODETYPE;
  NODETYPE = RECORD
   INFO1 : REAL;
   NEXTNODE : NODEPTR
   END;
```

The function:

```
FUNCTION COPYLST (HEAD : NODEPTR) : NODEPTR;
VAR
 Q : NODEPTR;
BEGIN
 IF HEAD = NIL THEN
  COPYLST := NIL
  (*TERMINATING CONDITION*)
 ELSE
  BEGIN
   NEW (Q);
   Q^.INFO1 := HEAD^.INFO1;
   Q^.NEXTNODE := COPYLST (HEAD^.NEXTNODE);
   COPYLST := Q
  END (*ELSE-BEGIN*)
 END;
```

Appendix: Files

In the sample programs in this book, the text files are INPUT and OUTPUT. INPUT and OUTPUT are predeclared. If you use these names for your input and output files, you don't have to declare them in your program. However, if there is input to your program, you usually must use the word INPUT as a program parameter and if there is output, you must use the word OUTPUT as a program parameter. With INPUT used as a program parameter, you can use the functions EOLN and EOF and the procedures READ and READLN without specifying any file names as parameters for the function or procedure. With OUTPUT used as a program parameter, you can use the procedures WRITE and WRITELN without specifying any file names for the procedure. With OUTPUT, you can also use the procedure PAGE, which instructs the computer to go to the beginning of the next page while printing, or to go to the beginning of a blank display on a monitor. You can do this with INPUT and OUTPUT files because READ (CHTR), for example, is really a shorthand way of saying:

```
CHTR := INPUT^ ;
GET (INPUT);
```

These two statements are the equivalent of reading CHTR. INPUT^ is a position pointer that reads the next available character. (On some systems, an upward-pointing arrow is used instead.) GET (INPUT) puts the character into the file-buffer variable and moves the pointer to the next available position. WRITE (CHTR), for example is shorthand for:

```
OUTPUT^ := CHTR;
PUT (OUTPUT);
```

OUTPUT^ points to the next available position. PUT (OUT-PUT) moves the character from the file-buffer variable into the output file and the value of the buffer variable becomes undefined.

You must move through your files position by position because all files in Standard Pascal are sequential. There are no random-access files in Standard Pascal. This means that in order to get to the Nth entry in a file, for example, you must first go through N − 1 entries. If file names are omitted in your program, it defaults to INPUT and OUTPUT as file names. You can, however, give your files other names that are declared in the VAR or TYPE section of your declarations.

To declare files:

```
TYPE
 TYPE-NAME = FILE OF FILE-TYPE;
VAR
 VARIABLE-NAME : TYPE-NAME;
```

For example:

```
TYPE
 FILETYPE = FILE OF INTEGER;
VAR
 NUMFILE : FILETYPE;
```

File items must all be of the same type. These can be of any type except files or a data structure that contains files. If a file is of type char, however, it can be declared as a file of type TEXT, which is predefined:

```
VAR
 VARIABLE-NAME : TEXT;
```

There are two built-in procedures used with declared files—RESET and REWRITE. RESET (FILE-NAME) opens a file so that you can read it. REWRITE (FILE-NAME) opens a file so that it can be written on. Except for INPUT and OUTPUT files, where this is done automatically, you have to either REWRITE or RESET the file before you use it.

The following programs illustrate the uses of GET, PUT, RESET, REWRITE, and pointers, and can be used for common file manipulations, such as displaying, copying, and merging files.

The first program illustrates the use of an input file, named MYFILE, which is being used instead of the file parameter INPUT. Notice that MYFILE is declared as TEXT in the VAR section of the program. In the RESET statement, the file pointer is set to the beginning of the file MYFILE. This program displays a file line for line:

```
PROGRAM DISPLAY (MYFILE,OUTPUT);
VAR
  MYFILE : TEXT;
  CHTR : CHAR;
BEGIN
  RESET (MYFILE);
  WHILE NOT EOF (MYFILE) DO
    BEGIN
      WHILE NOT EOLN (MYFILE) DO
        BEGIN
          READ (MYFILE, CHTR);
          WRITE (CHTR)
        END; (*WHILE-BEGIN*)
      READLN (MYFILE);
      WRITELN
    END (*WHILE-BEGIN*)
END.
```

A modified version of the program above can be used to copy MYFILE to another file called YOURFIL. You would need to REWRITE (YOURFIL) in order to open your file so that it could be written on. YOURFIL would then also be an argument for your WRITE and WRITELN statements:

```
PROGRAM COPY (MYFILE,YOURFIL);
VAR
  MYFILE,YOURFIL : TEXT;
  CHTR : CHAR;
```

```
BEGIN
  RESET (MYFILE);
  REWRITE (YOURFIL);
  WHILE NOT EOF (MYFILE) DO
    BEGIN
      WHILE NOT EOLN (MYFILE) DO
       BEGIN
         READ (MYFILE,CHTR);
         WRITE (YOURFIL,CHTR)
       END; (*WHILE-BEGIN*)
      READLN (MYFILE);
      WRITELN (YOURFIL)
    END (*WHILE-BEGIN*)
END.
```

The next program illustrates file merging, in this case integer files. They are both in order, and the larger merged file will be in order as well after the merge. Note that both FIRST and SECOND, the two files to be merged into LARGEFIL, are RESET before the merge.

```
PROGRAM MERGEFIL (FIRST,SECOND,LARGEFIL);
VAR
  FIRST,SECOND,LARGEFIL : FILE OF INTEGER;
BEGIN
  RESET (FIRST);
  RESET (SECOND);
  REWRITE (LARGEFIL);
  REPEAT
    IF FIRST^ <= SECOND^ THEN
      BEGIN
        LARGEFIL^ := FIRST^;
        GET (FIRST)
      END (*IF-BEGIN*)
    ELSE
      BEGIN
        LARGEFIL^ := SECOND^;
        GET (SECOND)
      END; (*ELSE-BEGIN*)
    PUT (LARGEFIL)
  UNTIL (EOF(FIRST)) OR (EOF(SECOND));
  WHILE NOT EOF (SECOND) DO
```

```
    BEGIN
      LARGEFIL^ : = SECOND^;
      PUT (LARGEFIL);
      GET (SECOND)
    END;
  WHILE NOT EOF (FIRST) DO
    BEGIN
      LARGEFIL^ : = FIRST^;
      PUT (LARGEFIL);
      GET (FIRST)
    END (*WHILE-BEGIN*)
END.
```

General Index

Index of Programs